THE WORLD BOOK

STUDENT DISCOVERY ENCYCLOPEDIA

THE WORLD BOOK
STUDENT DISCOVERY ENCYCLOPEDIA

SECOND EDITION

World Book, Inc.
a Scott Fetzer company
Chicago

V·W
X·Y
Z

12

For information about other World Book publications, visit our Web site **http://www.worldbook.com** or call **1-800-WORLDBK (967-5325).**

For information about sales to schools and libraries call **1-800-975-3250 (United States); 1-800-837-5365 (Canada).**

First edition published 2000. Second edition published 2007.

World Book, Inc.
233 N. Michigan Ave.
Chicago, IL 60601

Library of Congress Cataloging-in-Publication Data

The World Book student discovery encyclopedia.
p. cm.
Summary: "A 13-volume, illustrated, A-Z general reference encyclopedia for students with high interest, low reading levels, providing traditional features of adult reference works, plus activities, atlas of world maps, special articles, and cumulative index"--Provided by publisher.
Includes index.
ISBN-13: 978-0-7166-7414-6
ISBN-10: 0-7166-7414-9
1. Children's encyclopedias and dictionaries. I. World Book, Inc.
AG5.W838 2006
031--dc22 2006013004

Printed in the United States of America
2 3 4 5 6 7 8 9 12 11 10 09 08

Acknowledgments

The publishers gratefully acknowledge the courtesy of the following artists, photographers, publishers, institutions, agencies, and corporations for the illustrations in this volume. Credits should be read from top to bottom, left to right on their respective pages. All maps and all entries marked with an asterisk (*) denote illustrations that are the exclusive property of World Book, Inc. Artwork for all country flags was adapted from Cliptures™ by Dream Maker Software. State and province flags and seals were provided by the Flag Research Center unless otherwise credited. Artwork for state and province birds and floral emblems was provided by John Dawson*. History artwork for the state and province articles was provided by Kevin Chadwick*.

11 WORLD BOOK illustration by Zorica Dabich*

12-13 WORLD BOOK diagram by Arthur Grebetz*; WORLD BOOK photo*; Hallmark Historical Collection; © B&C Alexander, Photo Researchers

14-15 © Barsen Collection from Hulton Archive/Getty Images; © Stephen Dalton, Photo Researchers; Oil painting by G. P. A. Healy (Granger Collection)

16-17 © Barry Rowland, Stone/Getty Images; *Self Portrait in Grey Felt Hat* (1887) oil on canvas by Vincent Van Gogh, Van Gogh Museum, Amsterdam (SuperStock)

18-19 © Louis Renault, Photo Researchers; © Milind A. Ketkar, Dinodia Picture Agency; James Teason*

20-21 Eileen Mueller Neill*; James Teason*; James Teason*

22-23 © Cathy Melloan; Alex Ebel*; © David R. Frazier

24-25 © SuperStock

26-27 NASA; © Bullaty/Lomeo from Photo Researchers; Precision Graphics*; Harry McNaught*

28-29 © SuperStock

30-31 © Catherine Ursillo, Photo Researchers; Roberta Polfus*; Donald Moss*; Athos Menaboni*; WORLD BOOK illustration*

32-33 Granger Collection; Gwen Connelly*

34-35 © David R. Frazier; © Jon Riley, Stone/Getty Images; © SuperStock; Len Ebert*

36-37 © Joachim Messerschmidt, Bruce Coleman Inc.; © Wenzel Fischer, Taxi/Getty Images

38-39 © Manfred Gottschalk, Tom Stack & Associates; © Peter Rayner, Stone/Getty Images

40-41 © Christie's Images from SuperStock; Richard Hook*; Charles McBarron Jr.*

42-43 Charles McBarron Jr.*; Granger Collection

44-45 © Thomas Kitchin, Tom Stack & Associates; Eileen Mueller Neill*; © David R. Frazier

46-47 © Gene Ahrens, Bruce Coleman Inc.

48-49 © Hank Morgan, Photo Researchers; David Cunningham*

50-51 Margaret Ann Moran*; Margaret Ann Moran*; Margaret Ann Moran*; © Alfred Pasieka; © CNRI/SPL from Photo Researchers; © SPL from Photo Researchers; Rick Incrocci*

52-53 Leonard Morgan*; © Bob Daemmrich, Stone/Getty Images

54-55 © Greg Vaughn, Tom Stack & Associates; Granger Collection; © Mitchell Beasley Pub Ltd.; © David R. Frazier

56-57 Eileen Mueller Neill*; © Harold Simon, Tom Stack & Associates; Eileen Mueller Neill*; © Barry Griffiths, Photo Researchers; Eileen Mueller Neill*

58-59 © Tim Davis, Stone/Getty Images; © Tony Duffy, Allsport/Getty Images; WORLD BOOK diagram*; Eileen Mueller Neill*

60-61 Granger Collection; Larry Korb, Business Records Corporation; Guy Tudor*

62-63 Oil painting (1871) by Franz von Lenbach (Granger Collection)

64-65 © John Lawrence, Stone/Getty Images; Everett Collection; © Tom McHugh, Photo Researchers

66-67 © Thomas Kitchin, Tom Stack & Associates; Granger Collection; AP/Wide World; © Leonard Lee Rue III, Tom Stack & Associates

68-69 © David R. Frazier

70-71 Granger Collection; © Artstreet; © Wally McNamee, Woodfin Camp, Inc.; © Michael Ventura, Stone/Getty Images; Oil painting (1796) by Gilbert Stuart (Granger Collection)

72-73 © Henley & Savage, Stone/Getty Images; © Robert Daemmrich, Stone/Getty Images; Roberta Polfus*; © Ken G. Preston-Mafham, Animals Animals; Oxford Illustrators Ltd.*

74-75 WORLD BOOK illustrations; © Manfred Gottschalk, Tom Stack & Associates

76-77 © Inga Spence, Tom Stack & Associates; John Sandford*

78-79 Lawrie Taylor*; © George de Steinheil, SuperStock; © Peter Pearson, Stone/Getty Images

80-81 Kate Lloyd-Jones, Linden Artists*; Terry Hadler*; Terry Hadler*; © Bob and Clara Calhoun, Bruce Coleman Collection; © Bob and Clara Calhoun, Bruce Coleman Collection

82-83 John Sandford*

84-85 Eileen Mueller Neill*; AP/Wide World; Paul Turnbaugh*; National Oceanic and Atmospheric Administration; National Center for Atmospheric Research

86-87 © Frank Siteman; © Kindra Clineff, Stone/Getty Images; © Cathy Melloan; © G. Carleton Ray, Photo Researchers

88-89 Christabel King*; © Doug Pensinger, Allsport

90-91 © Terry Vine, Stone/Getty Images

92-93 © Bryan Allen, SuperStock

94-95 © SuperStock; © Tom Ulrich, Stone/Getty Images; Tony Gibbons*

96-97 Walter Linsenmaier*; Marion Pahl*

98-99 © Michael S. Nolan/Wildlife Images from Tom Stack & Associates; © Jen and Des Bartlett, Bruce Coleman Inc.; Marion Pahl*; Harry McNaught*

100-101 WORLD BOOK photo by Ralph J. Brunke*; James Teason*; © Keren Su, Corbis; © Ron Willocks, Animals Animals

102-103 Everett Collection; © Karen A. McCormack; Brown Brothers; Granger Collection

104-105 AP/Wide World; Michael Hampshire*; Everett Collection; Granger Collection

106-107 Everett Collection; Granger Collection; © Artstreet

108-109 © David R. Frazier; © S. Roberts, Everett Collection; Granger Collection; © George Hunter, Stone/Getty Images

110-111 © Phil Degginger, Stone/Getty Images

112-113 © Doris Dewitt, Stone/Getty Images; Colored engraving (late 1800's) by Howard Pyle (Granger Collection); © B. Seitz, Photo Researchers; Darrell Wiskur*

114-115 © Renee Lynn, Stone/Getty Images; Corbis/Bettmann; WORLD BOOK illustration*; AP/Wide World

Acknowledgments

116-117 WORLD BOOK photos by Chester B. Stem, Inc.*; WORLD BOOK illustration*; Oxford Illustrators Ltd.*; Guy Cohleach*; © Craig Jones, Allsport/Getty Images

118-119 © Hulton Archive/Getty Images; Bensen Studios*; Bensen Studios*; © David R. Frazier; Burlington Industries, Inc.; Burlington Industries, Inc.

120-121 Burlington Industries, Inc.; © David Crausby, Alamy Images; George Guzzi*

122-123 Tony Gibbons*; George Guzzi*

124-125 Tony Gibbons*; Granger Collection; Margaret Estey*; Cy Baker, Wildlife Art Ltd.*; Tony Gibbons*

126-127 Cy Baker, Wildlife Art Ltd.*; Guy Tudor*; University of Iowa

128-129 © C. H. Petit/Agence Vandystadt/ Photo Researchers; Richard Hook*; Library of Congress; Western Pennsylvania Conservancy

130-131 Everett Collection; Eileen Mueller Neill*

132-133 © John M. Burnley, Bruce Coleman Inc.

134-135 Saint Mary of Nazareth Hospital Center; © Lynn M. Stone, Animals Animals

136-137 Jill Coombs*; © Mark Douet, Stone/Getty Images; Eileen Mueller Neill*

138-139 © Cathy Melloan; © Ken M. Johns, Photo Researchers

140-141 © A. Tessore, SuperStock

142-143 © SuperStock; © Lindsay Hebbard, Corbis; © SuperStock; © Bill Aron, Stone/Getty Images

144-145 Eileen Mueller Neill*; © Reed Kaestner, Corbis; © Hulton Archive/Getty Images

146-147 © Stephen J. Krasemann, Photo Researchers

148-149 © Vince Streano, Stone/Getty Images

150-151 AP/Wide World

152-153 Granger Collection; James Teason*; Pat & Robin DeWitt*

154-155 © Thomas Kitchin, Tom Stack & Associates; Bensen Studios*

156-157 © Will and Deni McIntyre, Photo Researchers; WORLD BOOK photo*

158-159 Sydney Aquarium; Metropolitan Toronto Zoo

160 © David R. Frazier

Key to pronunciation

The World Book Student Discovery Encyclopedia provides pronunciation for many unusual or unfamiliar words. In the pronunciation, the words are divided into syllables and respelled according to the way each syllable sounds. The syllables appear in *italic* letters. For example, here are an article title and the respelled pronunciation for it:

Diplodocus (*duh PLAHD uh kuhs*)

The syllable or syllables that get the greatest emphasis when the word is spoken are in capital letters (*PLAHD*).

The World Book Student Discovery Encyclopedia uses a number of special characters and marks to give the correct spellings for many words and names in languages other than English. These marks have various meanings, according to the languages in which they are used. An acute accent mark (´) over an *e* in a French word indicates that the *é* is said *ay*. An acute accent mark over an *e* in a Spanish word indicates that the syllable containing the *é* has the main emphasis in the word.

The pronunciation key at the right shows how common word sounds are indicated by marks in *The World Book Dictionary* and by respelling in *The World Book Student Discovery Encyclopedia*. The key also shows examples of the *schwa*, or unaccented vowel sound. The schwa is represented by ə.

Letter or mark	As in	Respelling
a	h*a*t, m*a*p	a
a	*a*ge, f*a*ce	ay
ã	c*a*re, *ai*r	ai
ä	f*a*ther, f*a*r	ah
ch	*ch*ild, mu*ch*	ch
e	l*e*t, b*e*st	eh
e	*e*qual, s*ee*, mach*i*ne, cit*y*	ee
er	t*er*m, l*ear*n, s*ir*, w*or*k	ur
i	*i*t, p*i*n, h*y*mn	ih
i	*i*ce, f*i*ve	y or eye
k	*c*oat, loo*k*	k
o	h*o*t, r*o*ck	ah or o
o	*o*pen, g*o*, gr*ow*	oh
ô	*o*rder, *a*ll	aw
oi	*oi*l, v*oi*ce	oy
ou	h*ou*se, *ou*t	ow
s	*s*ay, ni*c*e	s
sh	*sh*e, vaca*ti*on	sh
u	c*u*p, b*u*tter, fl*oo*d	uh
u̇	f*u*ll, p*u*t, w*oo*d	u
ü	r*u*le, m*o*ve, f*oo*d,	oo
	m*u*sic	yoo
zh	plea*s*ure	zh
ə	*a*bout, *a*meba, tak*e*n, purp*le*, penc*i*l, lem*o*n, circ*u*s, curt*ai*n, Egypt*ia*n, sect*io*n, danger*ou*s	uh

How to use *The World Book Student Discovery Encyclopedia*

- Thousands of illustrations
- Guide words
- Phonetic spellings
- Related article lists
- Clear cross-references
- Fact boxes and timelines
- Special feature articles
- Hands-on activities

The World Book Student Discovery Encyclopedia is a general encyclopedia. It has information about people, places, things, events, and ideas. Entries are written in a way that makes them easy to understand.

Finding entries is easy, too. They are arranged in alphabetical order. There is also an index in volume 13. The index lists all the entries, as well as topics that are covered in the set but that are not themselves entries. Volume 13 has an atlas, too. It features maps of the world and maps of individual continents. Over 400 other maps are found throughout the set.

The many features of *Student Discovery* make it an encyclopedia that you can use for research as well as read just for fun.

Guide words At the top of each page is a guide word. Guide words help you quickly find the entry you are seeking.

Vatican City

Vatican City

Saint Peter's Basilica, Vatican City

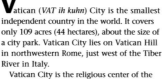

Vatican (*VAT ih kuhn*) City is the smallest independent country in the world. It covers only 109 acres (44 hectares), about the size of a city park. Vatican City lies on Vatican Hill in northwestern Rome, just west of the Tiber River in Italy.

Vatican City is the religious center of the Roman Catholic Church, the largest Christian church in the world. The ruler of Vatican City is the pope.

High stone walls surround most of the city. Several important buildings lie within the city walls, including Saint Peter's Basilica. Saint Peter's is one of the largest Christian churches in the world. A group of buildings called Vatican Palace contains the pope's apartment and Vatican government offices. Many beautiful works of art and important religious and historical papers are kept at the palace. Some of Michelangelo's greatest paintings decorate the ceiling and one large wall of the palace's Sistine Chapel. Michelangelo was one of the world's great artists.

According to old stories, Saint Peter, a follower of Jesus Christ, was killed on Vatican Hill and buried nearby. The early popes believed that a shrine, or place of worship, in the area marked the place where Saint Peter was buried, so they built Vatican City on that spot.

Beginning in the 700's, the popes ruled a region called the Papal States. In the 1800's, most of the land from the Papal States became part of Italy. In 1929, the rest became the independent country of Vatican City.

Other articles to read: **Christianity; Pope; Saint Peter's Basilica.**

Facts About Vatican City

Capital: Vatican City.
Area: 109 acres (44 hectares).
Population: 1,000.
Official language: Latin.
Climate: Temperate; mild, rainy winters with hot, dry summers.
Chief products: Postage stamps, publications, tourist souvenirs.
Form of government: Papacy.

Flag

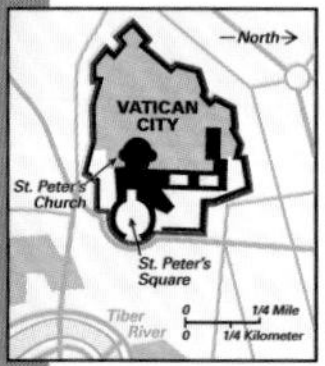

Vatican City lies inside the city of Rome in Italy.

VCR. See **Videotape recorder.**

18 The World Book Student Discovery Encyclopedia

Vedas

The Vedas (*VAY duhz*) are the oldest holy books of Hinduism, the major religion of India. There are four Vedas. They were written over a period of nearly 1,000 years, beginning about 3,400 years ago. However, they existed for hundreds of years before they were written down.

The Vedas talk about the Hindu gods and Brahman (*BRAH muhn*), Hinduism's highest spiritual being. They also talk about religious services and beliefs. Included with the Vedas are two later writings. These writings explain the meaning of ancient religious services and talk about the soul.

Hindu law allowed only certain people to hear the Vedas read out loud, so the works became surrounded by mystery. But the ideas presented in the Vedas spread throughout Indian culture.

The Vedas are the oldes Hinduism, the major relig There are four Vedas.

Vegetable

Vegetables are foods that come from plants. Vegetables are eaten raw or cooked. People can buy them fresh, canned, frozen, or dried. People eat vegetables in a main meal, in salads and soups, and as snacks. Vegetables provide people with many vitamins and minerals that help keep the body healthy.

Most vegetables come from plants that live for only one year or one growing season. Plant parts eaten as vegetables include bulbs, flowers, fruits, leaves, roots, seeds, stems, and tubers (*TOO buhrz*).

Vegetabl part of a p

Onions (bulbs)

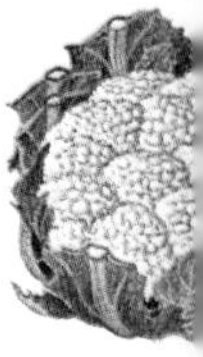

Cauliflower (flowers)

The World Book Student Discovery E

Cross-references The cross-references appear in heavy type—the same as article titles. For example, there is a cross-reference from **Earthworm** to **Worm.** This means if you look up **Earthworm,** you will be told to see the **Worm** article.

Related references The references at the bottom of many articles tell you what other articles to read to find out more or related information.

Pronunciations The phonetic spellings for many unusual or unfamiliar words are given. A key to the pronunciation is in the front of each volume.

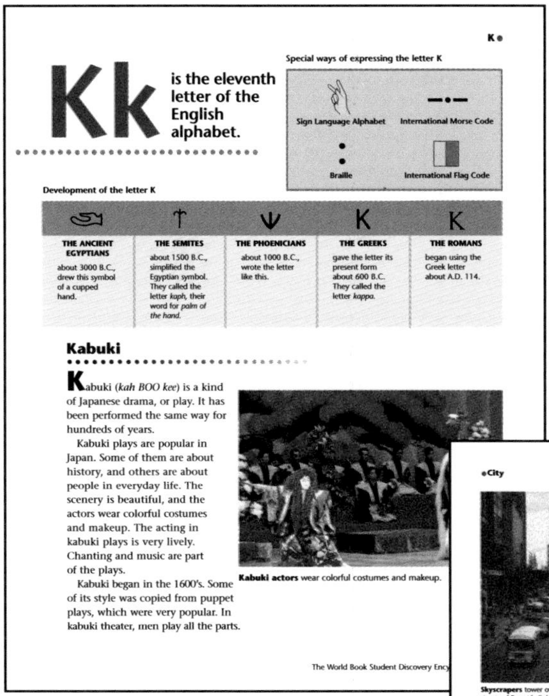

Kk is the eleventh letter of the English alphabet.

Special ways of expressing the letter K

Sign Language Alphabet | International Morse Code | Braille | International Flag Code

Development of the letter K

THE ANCIENT EGYPTIANS	THE SEMITES	THE PHOENICIANS	THE GREEKS	THE ROMANS
about 3000 B.C., drew this symbol of a cupped hand.	about 1500 B.C., simplified the Egyptian symbol. They called the letter *kaph*, their word for *palm of the hand.*	about 1000 B.C., wrote the letter like this.	gave the letter its present form about 600 B.C. They called the letter *kappa*.	began using the Greek letter about A.D. 114.

Kabuki

Kabuki (*kah BOO kee*) is a kind of Japanese drama, or play. It has been performed the same way for hundreds of years.

Kabuki plays are popular in Japan. Some of them are about history, and others are about people in everyday life. The scenery is beautiful, and the actors wear colorful costumes and makeup. The acting in kabuki plays is very lively. Chanting and music are part of the plays.

Kabuki began in the 1600's. Some of its style was copied from puppet plays, which were very popular. In kabuki theater, men play all the parts.

Kabuki actors wear colorful costumes and makeup.

The World Book Student Discovery Ency

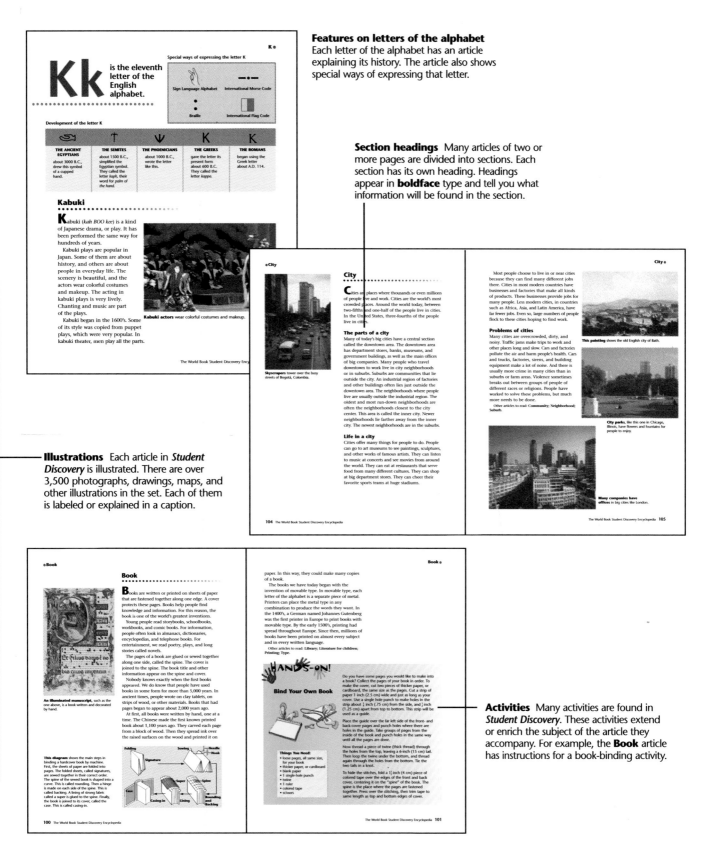

Features on letters of the alphabet Each letter of the alphabet has an article explaining its history. The article also shows special ways of expressing that letter.

Section headings Many articles of two or more pages are divided into sections. Each section has its own heading. Headings appear in **boldface** type and tell you what information will be found in the section.

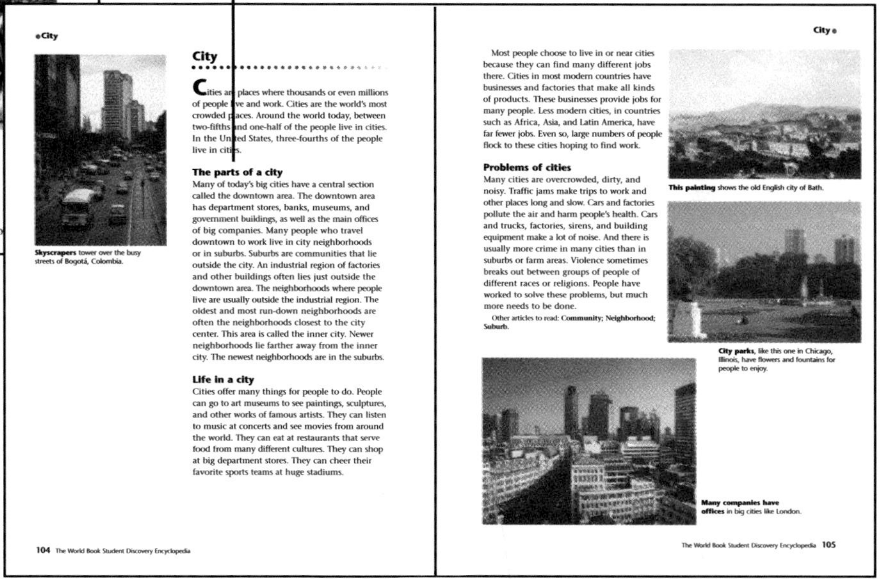

●City

City

Cities are places where thousands or even millions of people live and work. Cities are the world's most crowded places. Around the world today, between two-fifths and one-half of the people live in cities. In the United States, three-fourths of the people live in cities.

The parts of a city

Many of today's big cities have a central section called the downtown area. The downtown area has department stores, banks, museums, and government buildings, as well as the main offices of big companies. Many people who travel downtown to work live in city neighborhoods or in suburbs. Suburbs are communities that lie outside the city. An industrial region of factories and other buildings often lies just outside the downtown area. The neighborhoods where people live are usually outside the industrial region. The oldest and most run-down neighborhoods are often the neighborhoods closest to the city center. This area is called the inner city. Newer neighborhoods lie farther away from the inner city. The newest neighborhoods are in the suburbs.

Life in a city

Cities offer many things for people to do. People can go to art museums to see paintings, sculptures, and other works of famous artists. They can listen to music at concerts and see movies from around the world. They can eat at restaurants that serve food from many different cultures. They can shop at big department stores. They can cheer their favorite sports teams at huge stadiums.

Skyscrapers tower over the busy streets of Bogotá, Colombia.

104 The World Book Student Discovery Encyclopedia

City●

Most people choose to live in or near cities because they can find many different jobs there. Cities in most modern countries have businesses and factories that make all kinds of products. These businesses provide jobs for many people. Less modern cities, in countries such as Africa, Asia, and Latin America, have far fewer jobs. Even so, large numbers of people flock to these cities hoping to find work.

Problems of cities

Many cities are overcrowded, dirty, and noisy. Traffic jams make trips to work and other places long and slow. Cars and factories pollute the air and harm people's health. Cars and trucks, factories, sirens, and building equipment make a lot of noise. And there is usually more crime in many cities than in suburbs or farm areas. Violence sometimes breaks out between groups of people of different races or religions. People have worked to solve these problems, but much more needs to be done.

Other articles to read: **Community; Neighborhood; Suburb.**

This painting shows the old English city of Bath.

City parks, like this one in Chicago, Illinois, have flowers and fountains for people to enjoy.

Many companies have offices in big cities like London.

The World Book Student Discovery Encyclopedia 105

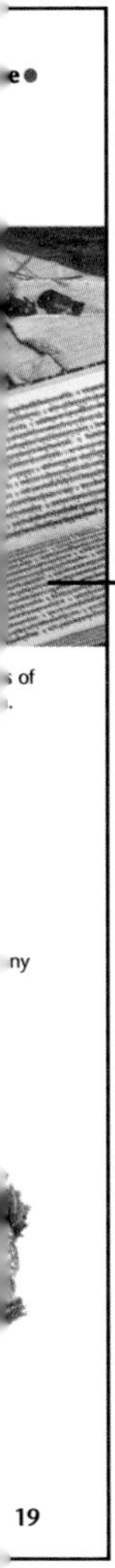

Illustrations Each article in *Student Discovery* is illustrated. There are over 3,500 photographs, drawings, maps, and other illustrations in the set. Each of them is labeled or explained in a caption.

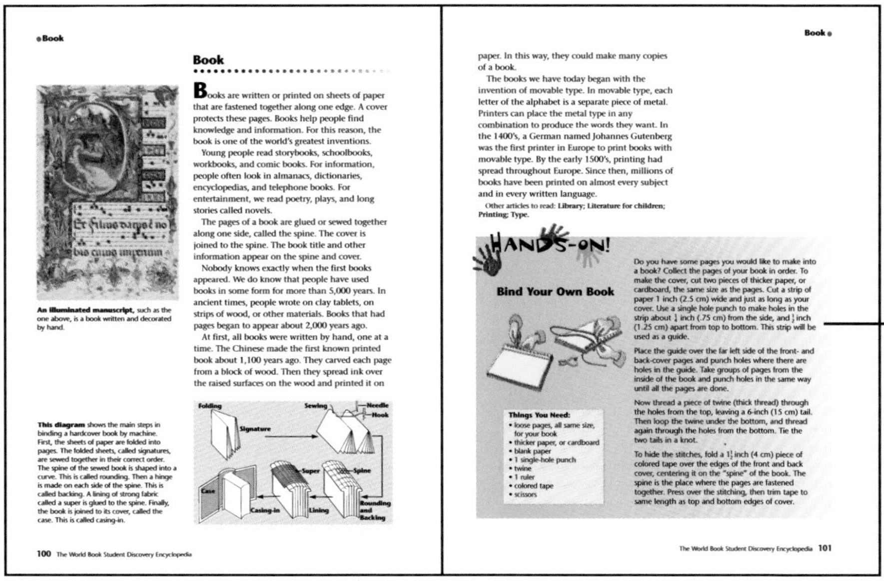

●Book

Book

Books are written or printed on sheets of paper that are fastened together along one edge. A cover protects these pages. Books help people find knowledge and information. For this reason, the book is one of the world's greatest inventions.

Young people read storybooks, schoolbooks, workbooks, and comic books. For information, people often look in almanacs, dictionaries, encyclopedias, and telephone books. For entertainment, we read poetry, plays, and long stories called novels.

The pages of a book are glued or sewed together along one side, called the spine. The cover is joined to the spine. The book title and other information appear on the spine and cover.

Nobody knows exactly when the first books appeared. We do know that people have used books in some form for more than 5,000 years. In ancient times, people wrote on clay tablets, on strips of wood, or other materials. Books that had pages began to appear about 2,000 years ago.

At first, all books were written by hand, one at a time. The Chinese made the first known printed book about 1,100 years ago. They carved each page from a block of wood. Then they spread ink over the raised surfaces on the wood and printed it on paper. In this way, they could make many copies of a book.

The books we have today began with the invention of movable type. In movable type, each letter of the alphabet is a separate piece of metal. Printers can place the metal type in any combination to produce the words they want. In the 1400's, a German named Johannes Gutenberg was the first printer in Europe to print books with movable type. By the early 1500's, printing had spread throughout Europe. Since then, millions of books have been printed on almost every subject and in every written language.

Other articles to read: **Library; Literature for children; Printing; Type.**

An illuminated manuscript, such as the one above, is a book written and decorated by hand.

This diagram shows the main steps in binding a hardcover book by machine. First, the sheets of paper are folded into pages. The folded sheets, called signatures, are sewed together in their correct order. The spine of the sewed book is shaped into a curve. This is called rounding. Then a hinge is made on each side of the spine. This is called backing. A lining of strong fabric called a super is glued to the spine. Finally, the book is joined to its cover, called the case. This is called casing-in.

Folding | Sewing | Needle | Hook | Signature | Super | Spine | Case | Casing-in | Lining | Rounding and Backing

100 The World Book Student Discovery Encyclopedia

Book●

HANDS-ON!

Bind Your Own Book

Do you have some pages you would like to make into a book? Collect the pages of your book in order. To make the cover, cut two pieces of thicker paper, or cardboard, the same size as the pages. Cut a strip of paper 1 inch (2.5 cm) wide and just as long as your cover. Use a single hole punch to make holes in the strip about ¼ inch (.75 cm) from the side, and ½ inch (1.25 cm) apart from top to bottom. This strip will be used as a guide.

Place the guide over the far left side of the front- and back-cover pages and punch holes where there are holes in the guide. Take groups of pages from the inside of the book and punch holes in the same way until all the pages are done.

Now thread a piece of twine (thick thread) through the holes from the top, leaving a 6-inch (15 cm) tail. Then loop the twine under the bottom, and thread again through the holes from the bottom. Tie the two tails in a knot.

To hide the stitches, fold a 1½ inch (4 cm) piece of colored tape over the edges of the front and back cover, centering it on the "spine" of the book. The spine is the place where the pages are fastened together. Press over the stitching, then trim tape to same length as top and bottom edges of cover.

Things You Need:
- loose pages, all same size, for your book
- thicker paper, or cardboard
- blank paper
- 1 single-hole punch
- twine
- 1 ruler
- colored tape
- scissors

The World Book Student Discovery Encyclopedia 101

Activities Many activities are found in *Student Discovery*. These activities extend or enrich the subject of the article they accompany. For example, the **Book** article has instructions for a book-binding activity.

How to use *Student Discovery*

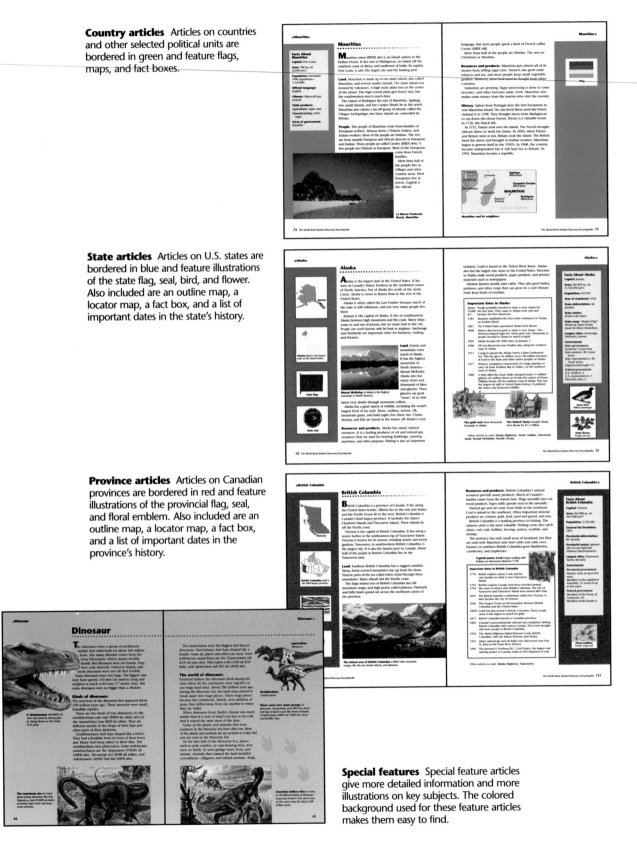

Country articles Articles on countries and other selected political units are bordered in green and feature flags, maps, and fact boxes.

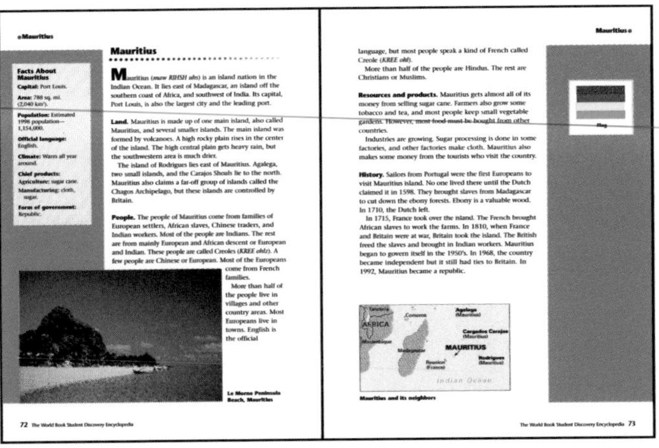

Mauritius
Facts About Mauritius
Mauritius and its neighbors
72 The World Book Student Discovery Encyclopedia
The World Book Student Discovery Encyclopedia 73

State articles Articles on U.S. states are bordered in blue and feature illustrations of the state flag, seal, bird, and flower. Also included are an outline map, a locator map, a fact box, and a list of important dates in the state's history.

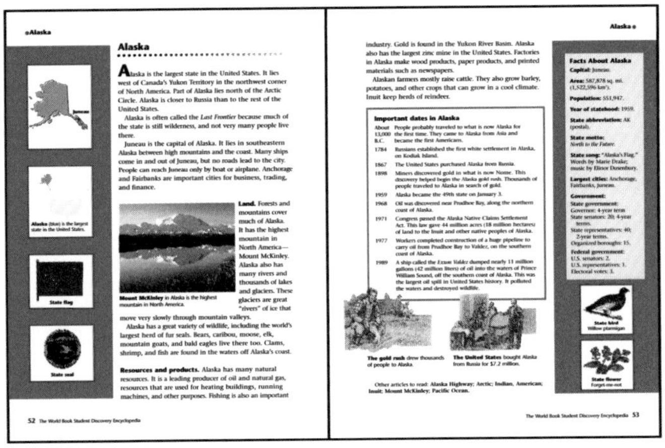

Province articles Articles on Canadian provinces are bordered in red and feature illustrations of the provincial flag, seal, and floral emblem. Also included are an outline map, a locator map, a fact box, and a list of important dates in the province's history.

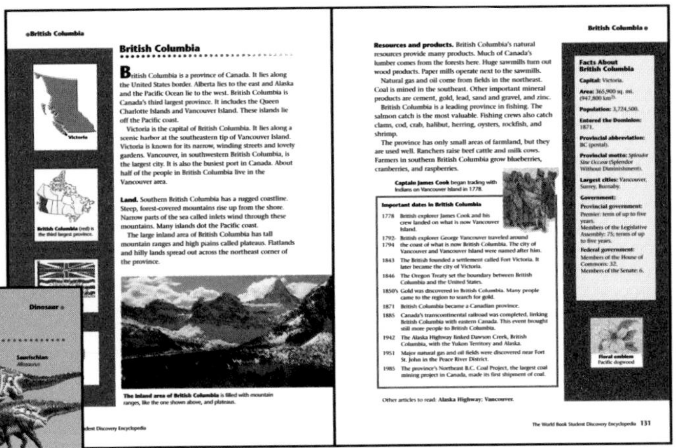

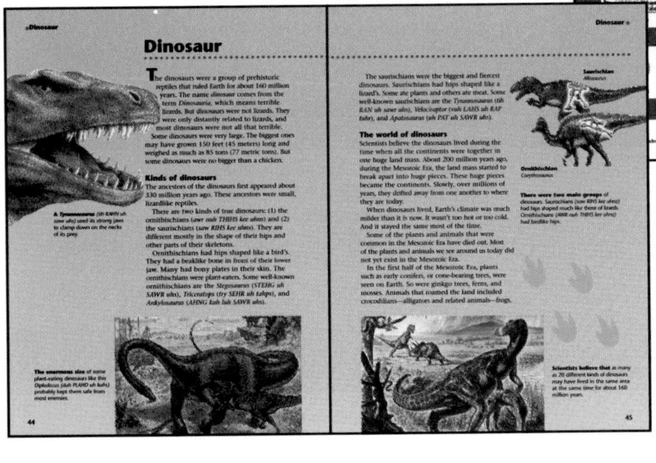

Special features Special feature articles give more detailed information and more illustrations on key subjects. The colored background used for these feature articles makes them easy to find.

Vv is the twenty-second letter of the English alphabet.

Special ways of expressing the letter V

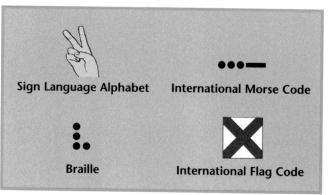

Sign Language Alphabet

• • • —
International Morse Code

Braille

International Flag Code

Development of the letter V

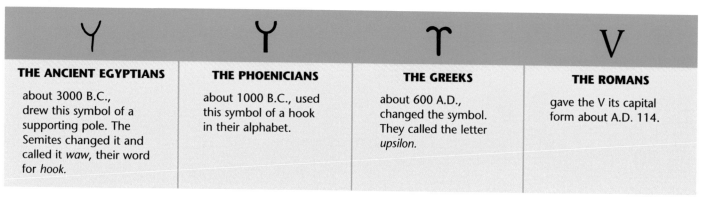

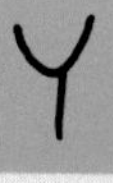			V
THE ANCIENT EGYPTIANS	**THE PHOENICIANS**	**THE GREEKS**	**THE ROMANS**
about 3000 B.C., drew this symbol of a supporting pole. The Semites changed it and called it *waw*, their word for *hook*.	about 1000 B.C., used this symbol of a hook in their alphabet.	about 600 A.D., changed the symbol. They called the letter *upsilon*.	gave the V its capital form about A.D. 114.

Vacuum

A vacuum (*VAK yoom*) is an area with nothing in it. However, there is no such thing as a complete vacuum because no one has ever been able to remove all of the air from any area. Scientists have been able to remove most of the air from certain areas, however, by creating specially sealed containers. So when scientists talk about a vacuum, they are talking about an area in a container with most of the air taken out.

We use vacuums in many ways. A vacuum cleaner uses a vacuum to suck up air. Vacuum bottles, such as Thermos bottles, have a vacuum between their double walls to help keep drinks hot or cold. Foods dry out more quickly in a vacuum, so companies that sell food products use vacuums to make instant foods, such as soup and powdered milk.

Other articles to read: **Vacuum cleaner.**

A vacuum makes this meat baster work. Squeezing the bulb, *left,* pushes air from the tube. When the bulb is released, *right,* fluid pushes into the tube to fill the vacuum.

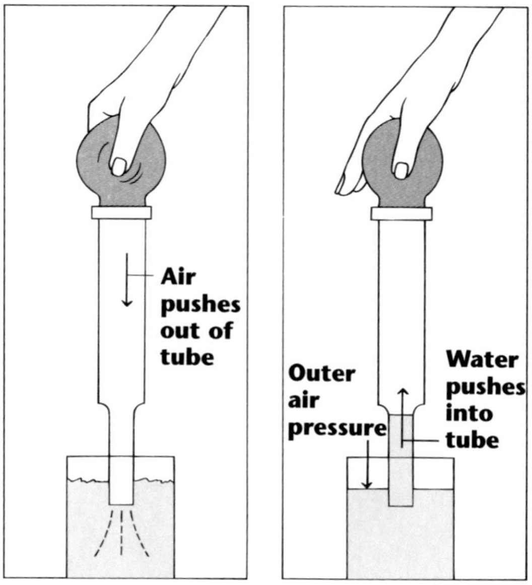

Vacuum cleaner

A vacuum cleaner is a machine that sucks up dirt and dust. People use vacuum cleaners to remove dirt from floors, furniture, curtains, and other things.

A vacuum cleaner sucks up air through a fan. As the fan spins, it pushes air away from it. Air from the outside then rushes in to fill the space. As the air flows in, it pulls dirt along with it. A cloth or paper bag catches the dirt, and the cleaned air is blown out of the machine. The bag must be emptied or changed regularly. In some vacuum cleaners, the dirt flows into a tank of water instead of a bag.

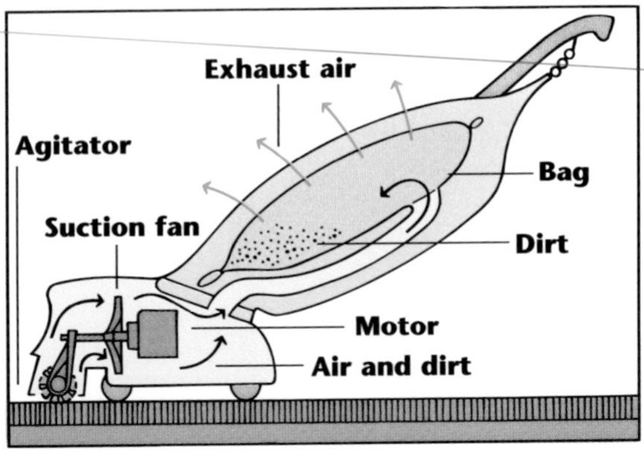

Upright vacuum cleaner

Valentine's Day

Valentine's Day is a special day that is celebrated on February 14. People in the United States, Canada, Australia, and most European countries celebrate Valentine's Day. Many people send greeting cards called valentines to sweethearts, friends, and family members. Some people send flowers or candy to their wives, husbands, friends, or sweethearts. Many valentine candy boxes are heart-shaped and tied with red ribbon.

Valentines include both humorous and romantic cards. Special ones are printed for sweethearts and for husbands, wives, and relatives. Many cards say "Be my valentine."

No one knows for sure how Valentine's Day started. The idea of sending greetings on Valentine's Day goes back hundreds of years. Some people think this idea may have come from events in the life of Saint Valentine, a Christian saint. One story says that Valentine was a friend of many children. The Romans put him in prison because he believed in Jesus Christ and would not pray to Roman gods. The children missed Valentine and tossed loving notes to him through the windows of his jail cell. This story may explain why people send messages on Valentine's Day.

Valentine cards were first sold in the early 1800's. Many of them were blank inside, leaving space for the sender to write a message. Kate Greenaway, a British artist, became famous for her valentines in the late 1800's. Many of her cards had pictures of happy children and lovely gardens.

Valentines by Kate Greenaway, a British artist, showed garden scenes. This card was printed in the 1880's.

Valley

A valley is a natural dip in the ground. Valleys run through hills, mountains, and flat areas of land called plains. Valleys are found on the ocean floor, too. Some valleys are narrow, and some are wide. Rivers and streams often flow through valleys. Many valleys have good soil for farmland.

Most valleys form when the running water of a river wears away the earth along its banks. A slowly moving sheet of ice called a glacier (*GLAY shuhr*) can scrape out a U-shaped valley in mountains. A rift valley may form when part of the earth's crust sinks.

Other articles to read: **Glacier.**

The Kugalik River Valley in Canada

Vampire

A vampire is a dead person who is said to come to life to suck people's blood at night. Vampires are not real, but some people believe in them.

There are many stories and folk tales about vampires. Some stories tell about vampires biting the neck of sleeping people and sucking their blood. These people die and become vampires themselves. According to legends, a vampire can be destroyed only if a person pounds a wooden stick through its heart.

Most vampire stories come from Eastern European and Balkan countries, such as Albania, Greece, Hungary, and Romania. The most famous vampire story is *Dracula* (1897) by the English author Bram Stoker. The character of Dracula is based on a real person, a cruel prince who lived in what is now Romania.

Dracula is the most famous vampire. There have been many movies about him in many different languages.

Vampire bat

Vampire bat

A vampire bat is a small flying animal that attacks other animals and drinks their blood. There are several kinds of vampire bats. The best known is the common vampire bat. It is about 3 inches (8 centimeters) long and has sharp, triangle-shaped front teeth. It has reddish-brown fur, and its wings are covered with smooth skin.

Most vampire bats live in Central America and warm, wet parts of North and South America. They attack horses, cattle, birds, and other warm-blooded animals. Vampire bats sometimes attack people who are sleeping. The bite itself is harmless and soon heals, but vampire bats may carry a deadly disease called rabies (*RAY beez*). A person can die from rabies if the disease is not treated.

Van Buren, Martin

Martin Van Buren (1782-1862) was the eighth president of the United States. He served from 1837 to 1841. During his years as president, the nation suffered its first great depression, the Panic of 1837. The depression brought money problems to millions of people.

Martin Van Buren

Martin Van Buren was born in Kinderhook, New York. At the age of 14, he began to study law. After finishing his studies in New York City, Van Buren opened a law office in Kinderhook. He married Hannah Hoes in 1807. She died in 1819.

Before becoming president, Van Buren worked in government jobs in New York. Later, he was elected a United States senator and then governor of New York. President Andrew Jackson made Van Buren U.S. secretary of state in 1829. The secretary of state helps the president deal with other countries. Van Buren was elected vice president under Jackson in 1832.

In 1836, Van Buren was elected president. The depression was only one of many problems at that time. In 1839, the United States and Canada could not agree on the border between the U.S. state of Maine and the Canadian province of New Brunswick. Van Buren settled the problem peacefully, but people did not pay much attention to his work. Fights between groups who wanted to keep slavery and those who wanted to make slavery against the law were also common at the time.

In 1840, Van Buren lost the election for a second term as president. He returned to his home in Lindenwald near Kinderhook. Van Buren ran for president again in 1848, but he lost.

Vancouver

Vancouver is Canada's busiest port. It is also the largest city and the major cultural and industrial center of British Columbia. The Coast Mountains tower in the background.

Vancouver (*van KOO vuhr*) is the largest city in British Columbia and Canada's busiest port. It lies in southwestern British Columbia, about 25 miles (40 kilometers) north of the border between Canada and the United States.

The city is a center of business, culture, and industry. Colorful totem poles made by American Indians stand in Stanley Park, one of the largest city parks in Canada. About half of all the people in British Columbia live in the Vancouver area.

The city was named after Captain George Vancouver, a British explorer who sailed into the town's harbor in 1792. People first settled in the area in 1865. Forests and the natural harbor helped the area grow as a lumber town and seaport. In 1886, Vancouver became a city.

Van Gogh, Vincent

Vincent van Gogh is shown in this self-portrait, or picture he painted of himself.

Vincent van Gogh (*VIHN sehnt van GOH*) (1853-1890) is one of the most famous painters in modern art. During his lifetime, however, he was not well known, and he sold only one painting.

Van Gogh was born in the Netherlands. He began painting as a job in 1880. After he moved to Paris in 1886, he experimented with impressionism (*ihm PREHSH uh nihz uhm*) and other modern-art styles. Impressionism is a style of painting that tries to show what the eye sees at a glance.

In 1888, van Gogh moved to Arles in southern France. The beautiful surroundings gave him the idea to use bright colors and strong brushstrokes. But van Gogh was mentally ill and unhappy. In 1888, he cut off his earlobe after a fight with the painter Paul Gauguin. Van Gogh killed himself in 1890.

Vanuatu

Vanuatu *(VAH noo AH too)* is an island country in the southwest Pacific Ocean. Eighty islands make up the nation of Vanuatu. Port-Vila, on the island of Efate *(eh FAH tay),* is the nation's capital and largest town.

The islands of Vanuatu form a Y-shaped chain. Tropical rain forests cover much of the northern islands. Grasslands are common on the southern islands. Mountains rise on many islands. Several islands have active volcanoes.

Most of Vanuatu's people are a Pacific Island people called Melanesians *(mehl uh NEE zhuhnz).* Asians, Europeans, and Polynesians also live there. Most of the people are Christians.

More than 100 languages are spoken in Vanuatu. Bislama, a language that combines mainly English words with Melanesian grammar words, is commonly spoken throughout the country.

Most of the people of Vanuatu live in villages and farm for a living. The country's farmers grow nearly all their own food. Some produce dried coconut meat called copra *(KAHP ruh),* coffee beans, and cacao for sale. Cacao beans are used to make chocolate. The country also makes money from visitors who come to enjoy its sandy beaches and sparkling blue waters.

Melanesians have lived in what is now Vanuatu for at least 3,000 years. People from Britain and France began moving to the islands during the 1840's. From 1906 to 1980, Britain and France governed the islands together. In 1980, the islands became the independent nation of Vanuatu.

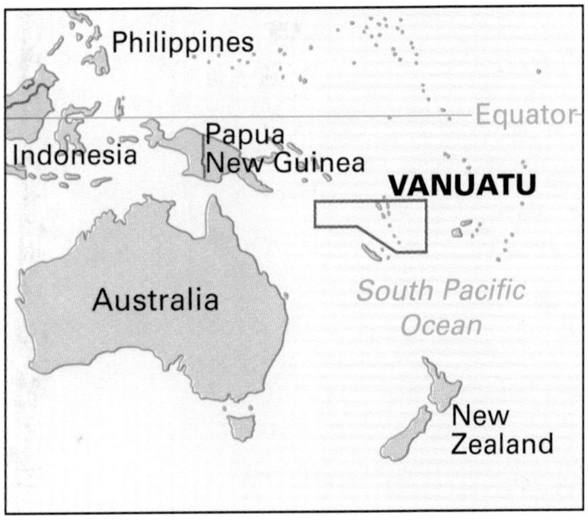

Vanuatu and its neighbors

Facts About Vanuatu

Capital: Port-Vila.

Area: 4,700 sq. mi. (12,200 km²).

Population: Estimated 2006 population—218,000.

Official languages: Bislama, English, French.

Climate: Hot and rainy, sometimes with cyclones.

Chief products:
Agriculture: cacao, chickens, coffee beans, copra, fish, fruit, hogs, meat, vegetables.

Form of government: Republic.

Flag

Vatican City

Saint Peter's Basilica, Vatican City

Vatican (*VAT ih kuhn*) City is the smallest independent country in the world. It covers only 109 acres (44 hectares), about the size of a city park. Vatican City lies on Vatican Hill in northwestern Rome, just west of the Tiber River in Italy.

Vatican City is the religious center of the Roman Catholic Church, the largest Christian church in the world. The ruler of Vatican City is the pope.

High stone walls surround most of the city. Several important buildings lie within the city walls, including Saint Peter's Basilica. Saint Peter's is one of the largest Christian churches in the world. A group of buildings called Vatican Palace contains the pope's apartment and Vatican government offices. Many beautiful works of art and important religious and historical papers are kept at the palace. Some of Michelangelo's greatest paintings decorate the ceiling and one large wall of the palace's Sistine Chapel. Michelangelo was one of the world's great artists.

According to old stories, Saint Peter, a follower of Jesus Christ, was killed on Vatican Hill and buried nearby. The early popes believed that a shrine, or place of worship, in the area marked the place where Saint Peter was buried, so they built Vatican City on that spot.

Beginning in the 700's, the popes ruled a region called the Papal States. In the 1800's, most of the land from the Papal States became part of Italy. In 1929, the rest became the independent country of Vatican City.

Other articles to read: **Christianity; Pope; Saint Peter's Basilica.**

Facts About Vatican City

Capital: Vatican City.

Area: 109 acres (44 hectares).

Population: 1,000.

Official language: Latin.

Climate: Temperate; mild, rainy winters with hot, dry summers.

Chief products: Postage stamps, publications, tourist souvenirs.

Form of government: Papacy.

Flag

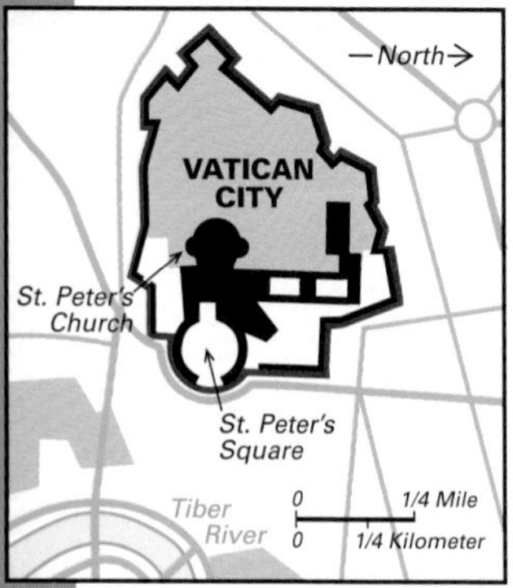

Vatican City lies inside the city of Rome in Italy.

VCR. See **Videotape recorder.**

Vedas

The Vedas (*VAY duhz*) are the oldest holy books of Hinduism, the major religion of India. There are four Vedas. They were written over a period of nearly 1,000 years, beginning about 3,400 years ago. However, they existed for hundreds of years before they were written down.

The Vedas talk about the Hindu gods and Brahman (*BRAH muhn*), Hinduism's highest spiritual being. They also talk about religious services and beliefs. Included with the Vedas are two later writings. These writings explain the meaning of ancient religious services and talk about the soul.

Hindu law allowed only certain people to hear the Vedas read out loud, so the works became surrounded by mystery. But the ideas presented in the Vedas spread throughout Indian culture.

The Vedas are the oldest holy books of Hinduism, the major religion of India. There are four Vedas.

Vegetable

Vegetables are foods that come from plants. Vegetables are eaten raw or cooked. People can buy them fresh, canned, frozen, or dried. People eat vegetables in a main meal, in salads and soups, and as snacks. Vegetables provide people with many vitamins and minerals that help keep the body healthy.

Most vegetables come from plants that live for only one year or one growing season. Plant parts eaten as vegetables include bulbs, flowers, fruits, leaves, roots, seeds, stems, and tubers (*TOO buhrz*).

Vegetables can be any part of a plant.

Onions (bulbs)

Cauliflower (flowers)

HANDS-ON!

Veggie Dip Ships

This vegetable dip is hearty enough to feed a group of hungry sailors!

With a plastic knife, cut out the center of each roll. Ask an adult for help with cutting.

Have an adult help you cut the cheese slices in quarters, the celery in strips, and the rest of the vegetables into slices.

Now, build your dip ships. Fill the rolls with dip. Place veggie circles in rows in the dip. Prop celery sticks on the sides to look like oars.

Thread a toothpick through each cheese quarter to make a sail. Stick the sail into the ship. Your veggie dip ships are ready to serve.

Things You Need:

- long sandwich rolls
- container of vegetable dip
- sliced Swiss cheese
- toothpicks
- assorted vegetables (carrots, cauliflower, cucumbers, celery, and zucchini squash)

Bulbs have many leaves around a short stem. The base of these leaves is large and grows underground. Garlic, leeks, onions, and shallots are vegetable bulbs.

The flowers most often used as vegetables are broccoli and cauliflower. Fruits also come from the flowers of plants. Fruits are the parts that enclose the seeds. The fruits of vegetable plants include cucumbers, eggplants, peppers, pumpkins, snap beans, and tomatoes.

Leaves eaten as vegetables include those of Brussels sprouts, cabbage, kale, lettuce, mustard, and spinach. Some of these vegetables are cooked, and others are eaten raw in salads. Celery and rhubarb are leafstalks.

Several kinds of roots are eaten as vegetables. Some, like sweet potatoes, branch out and spread

Eggplant (fruit)

Spinach (leaves)

Potatoes (tubers)

sideways. Others are parts of large roots that grow straight down. These large roots include beets, carrots, parsnips, radishes, rutabagas, and turnips.

People eat the seeds of plants when they eat garden peas, kidney beans, lima beans, navy beans, and sweet corn. Some seeds, such as kidney beans and navy beans, are picked after they become hard. Other seeds, such as garden peas and sweet corn, are picked when they are still soft.

Stems support the leaves, flowers, and fruits of a plant. Two stems that are often eaten as vegetables are asparagus and kohlrabi (*KOHL RAH bee*). Asparagus stems are tall and slender. Kohlrabi plants have large, bulblike stems.

Most tubers are thick stems that grow underground. The most popular tubers are potatoes and Jerusalem artichokes.

The three basic steps in growing vegetables are planting, caring for the crop, and harvesting, or picking, the vegetable. Vegetables that are raised for sale in stores must also be packed and shipped. Most growers use machines for these tasks.

China grows more vegetables than any other country. California produces about one-third of all the vegetables grown in the United States. Ontario grows more vegetables than any other province in Canada.

Other articles to read: **Farm and farming; Gardening; Nutrition; Vegetarianism**; and those on individual vegetables.

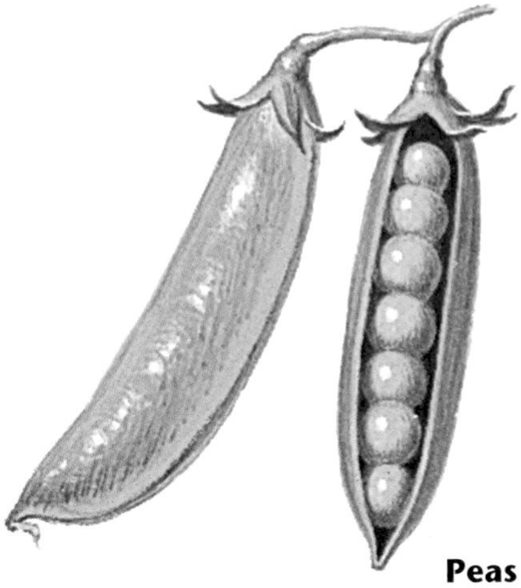

Peas (seeds)

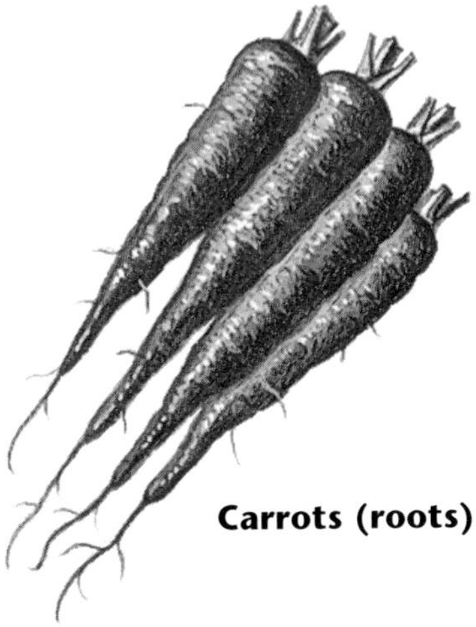

Carrots (roots)

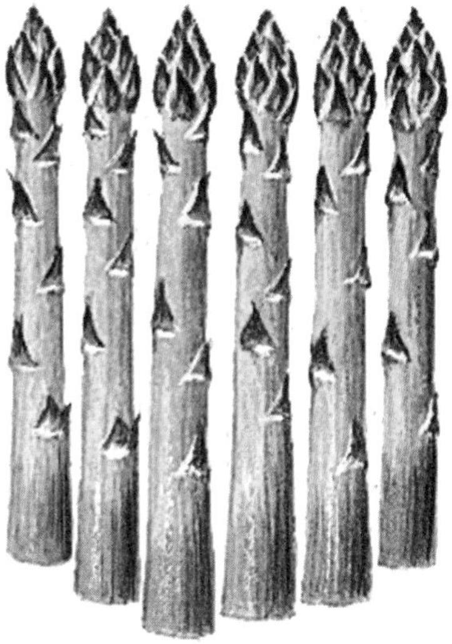

Asparagus (stems)

Vegetarianism

Vegetarianism (*VEHJ uh TAIR ee uhn ihzm*) is the practice of not eating meat. Some vegetarians do not eat meat, milk, eggs, or any dishes made with milk and eggs because these foods come from animals. Other vegetarians do not eat eggs, but they drink milk and eat milk products, such as butter and cheese.

A good vegetarian diet includes many fruits, grains, and vegetables and is low in fat.

Vegetarianism can be a healthy way of eating. A good vegetarian diet includes many fruits, grains, and vegetables and is low in fat. However, meat is an important food. It contains protein and other important nutrients, the things people need to stay healthy. So vegetarians must make sure to eat foods that contain proteins, vitamins, and minerals. Milk and eggs are good sources of protein and other nutrients. Beans, nuts, and peas also contain protein. When eaten with certain other foods, such as brown rice, they provide as much nourishment as meat. Some vegetarians take vitamins to make sure they get all the nutrients they need.

Most vegetarians do not eat meat because they believe it is wrong to kill animals for food. Some vegetarians do not eat meat for religious reasons. Many vegetarians also think that eating meat is unhealthy. Other vegetarians believe that eating meat is wasteful. They point out that the grain used to raise a cow can feed more people than the meat that comes from that cow.

Velcro

Velcro is a fastener made of tiny hooks and loops. It is used in clothing, shoes, sports and medical equipment, and inside automobiles and airplanes. A Swiss engineer named Georges de Mestral got the idea for Velcro in the 1940's while pulling burs from his dog's fur. Burs are prickly seed coverings that stick to fur or cloth.

A Velcro fastener is made up of two strips that are glued or sewn onto fabrics or other objects to be joined. Tiny hooks made of strong thread cover one of the strips. A fuzzy mat of loops made of thinner threads covers the other strip. When the strips are pressed together, the hooks attach to the loops and the two strips stick together. The strips can be pulled apart and used again and again.

A Velcro fastener is made up of two strips. Tiny hooks cover one strip, and fuzzy loops cover the other strip. When the strips are pressed together, the hooks attach to the loops, and the two strips stick together.

Velociraptor

The velociraptor (*vuh LAHS uh RAP tuhr*) was a meat-eating dinosaur. It lived about 80 million years ago in what is now Mongolia and northern China.

The velociraptor grew about 20 inches (50 centimeters) tall at the hips and about 6 feet (1.8 meters) long. It had sharp teeth, powerful legs, and two giant toe claws. The velociraptor was a fast runner. It probably used its speed to catch other dinosaurs and then killed them with its toe claws.

Velociraptor

In 1971, scientists found an interesting fossil skeleton of a velociraptor in the Gobi Desert in Mongolia. The skeleton's arms still held the skull of another dinosaur. The creatures may have been buried alive as they fought during a sandstorm.

Facts About Venezuela

Capital: Caracas.

Area: 352,144 sq. mi. (912,050 km²).

Population: Estimated 2006 population—25,045,000.

Official language: Spanish.

Climate: Hot. Cooler in the mountains. Rainfall is heavy in the far west and south and lightest along much of the coast.

Chief products:

Agriculture: bananas, beef cattle, chickens and eggs, coffee, milk.

Manufacturing: aluminum, petrochemicals, pig iron, processed foods, refined petroleum, steel.

Mining: alumina, coal, iron ore, natural gas, petroleum.

Form of government: Federal republic.

Flag

Venezuela

Venezuela (*VEHN ih ZWAY luh*) is a South American country. It lies on the north coast of South America along the Caribbean Sea. Venezuela borders Guyana on the east, Brazil on the south, and Colombia on the west. Caracas (*kuh RAH kuhs*) is the capital and largest city.

Land. Mountain ranges stretch across much of northern Venezuela. Lake Maracaibo (*MAR uh KY boh*) in northwestern Venezuela is the biggest lake in South America. This area has the largest known amounts of oil in South America. Angel Falls in eastern Venezuela is the world's highest waterfall. It falls 3,212 feet (979 meters).

A flat grassland spreads across central Venezuela. Large cattle ranches and farms cover much of the region. Important oil fields lie in the eastern part of the grassland.

Low mountains and tropical forests cover much of the southern part of the country. The northeast has low mountains and gently sloping hills.

People. Hundreds of years ago, many groups of American Indians lived in what is now Venezuela. In the 1500's, the Spanish took over the lands of many of these peoples. They also brought black slaves from Africa to the area. Many American Indians, Spaniards, and blacks married one another and raised families. Today, more than half of Venezuela's people come from these mixed families. Most of Venezuela's people live in cities and towns.

Almost all of Venezuela's people speak Spanish, the country's official language. Some American Indians speak their own languages. Most of the people are Roman Catholics.

Common foods in Venezuela include

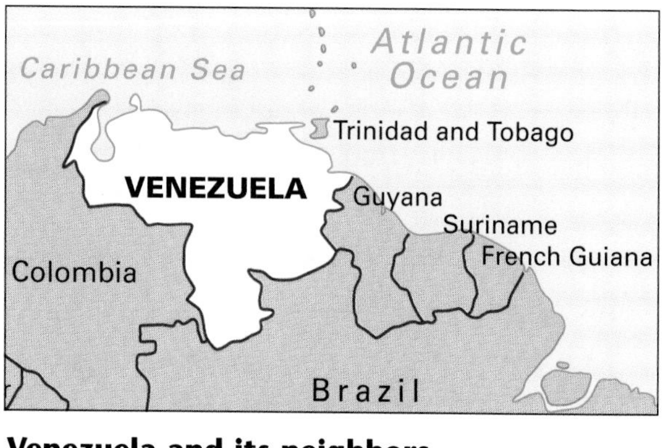

Venezuela and its neighbors

black beans, a kind of banana called plantains, and rice. The foods are usually eaten with beef, pork, chicken, or fish. Baseball and soccer are the most popular sports that people in Venezuela watch. The people also enjoy music and dancing.

Resources and products. Venezuela is one of the world's biggest producers and sellers of petroleum, or oil. Before its oil industry began to grow quickly in the 1920's, Venezuela was a poor country. Since then, Venezuela has become one of the richest countries in South America.

Venezuela also has huge amounts of coal, diamonds, gold, and other minerals. Its factories produce aluminum, cement, cloth, food products, and steel.

More than half of Venezuela's workers have jobs in service businesses. Some work as teachers and doctors, for example, and others have jobs in stores, hotels, and restaurants.

Hacha Falls in Canaima National Park, Venezuela

History. The Italian ship captain Christopher Columbus was the first European to visit Venezuela. He landed in the area in 1498 on his third voyage to the New World. It was his first landing on the mainland of the Americas.

In northwestern Venezuela, American Indians built their houses on poles over the waters of the Gulf of Venezuela and Lake Maracaibo. When European explorers saw this, it reminded them of the Italian city of Venice, where buildings stood along the water. They named the area *Venezuela,* which is Spanish for *Little Venice.*

Spain ruled Venezuela for about 300 years. In 1811, Venezuela declared its independence from Spain. In 1819, Venezuela became part of Gran Colombia, a country that also included what are now Colombia, Ecuador, and Panama. Venezuela broke away from Gran Colombia in 1829 and became a separate independent country in 1830.

Venice

Venice (*VEHN ihs*) is one of the world's most famous and unusual cities. It lies on about 120 islands in the Adriatic Sea, about $2\frac{1}{2}$ miles (4 kilometers) off the coast of Italy. Venice has canals, or waterways, instead of streets. People there get around on boats instead of cars and buses. Motorboats are the main way to travel. But passengers are also carried in gondolas (*GAHN doh luhz*). Gondolas are long, thin boats pushed through the water with long oars. More than 400 bridges cross the canals and connect the main islands of Venice. Venice has many beautiful stone buildings and fine works of art.

Today, Venice is in danger of being destroyed because of floods and dirty air and water. People from many parts of the world are working on ways to save Venice.

In Venice, canals take the place of streets, and boats are used for travel. Most of the buildings that line the canals are hundreds of years old.

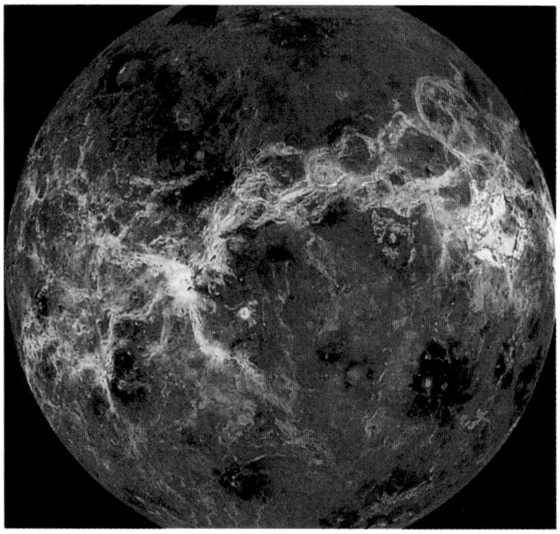

Venus is surrounded by thick acid clouds. Astronomers cannot see its surface even with telescopes. This picture was made using radar waves and photos taken from cameras that landed on Venus.

Venus

Venus is a planet. It is closer to the sun than any other planet except Mercury. Venus is known as Earth's "twin" because the two planets are about the same size. No other planet is nearer to Earth than Venus.

From Earth, Venus looks brighter than any other planet or even any star in the sky. At certain times of the year, Venus is the first planet or star that can be seen in the western sky in the evening. At other times, it is the last planet or star that can be seen in the eastern sky in the morning. When Venus is bright, it can be seen even in daylight.

Mountains and volcanoes rise over much of the planet, and canyons and craters mark its surface. The plants and animals that live on Earth could not live on Venus. Venus is covered with thick clouds of deadly sulfuric acid. It is also much too hot. The temperature on the surface of Venus is about 860 °F (460 °C), hotter than most ovens. Scientists do not think anything lives on Venus.

Scientists have sent spacecraft to Venus to explore the planet. The first spacecraft to pass near Venus was Mariner 2 in 1962. In 2005, the European Space Agency launched the Venus Express probe. The probe was designed to study Venus's atmosphere and to scan the planet's surface for volcanoes. The probe began orbiting the planet in April 2006.

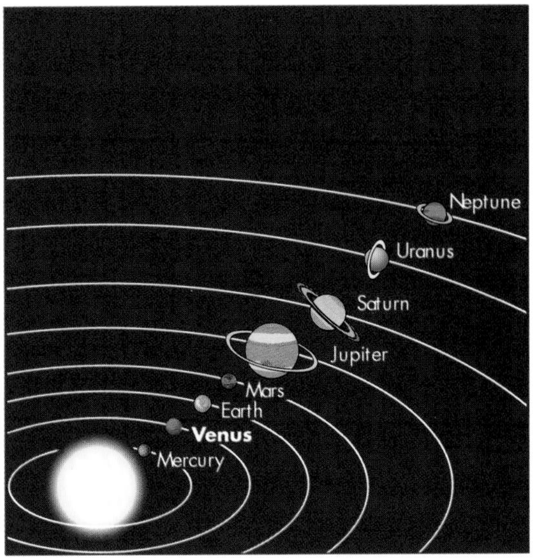

Venus is the second planet from the sun. Venus is known as Earth's "twin" because the two planets are about the same size.

Venus's-flytrap

The Venus's-flytrap (*VEE nuhs sihz FLY trap*) is a plant that traps insects for food. It is found along the coasts of North Carolina and South Carolina. Venus's-flytrap grows in soft, wet areas called bogs.

Venus's-flytrap grows about 12 inches (30 centimeters) high. It has small white flowers, and leaves that work like a steel trap. These leaves have hairs on them that feel the slightest touch. When an insect touches one of the hairs, the leaves close up tight and trap the insect inside. A special liquid in the leaf helps the plant break down the soft parts of the insect as food. After a leaf has caught several insects, it dries up and dies.

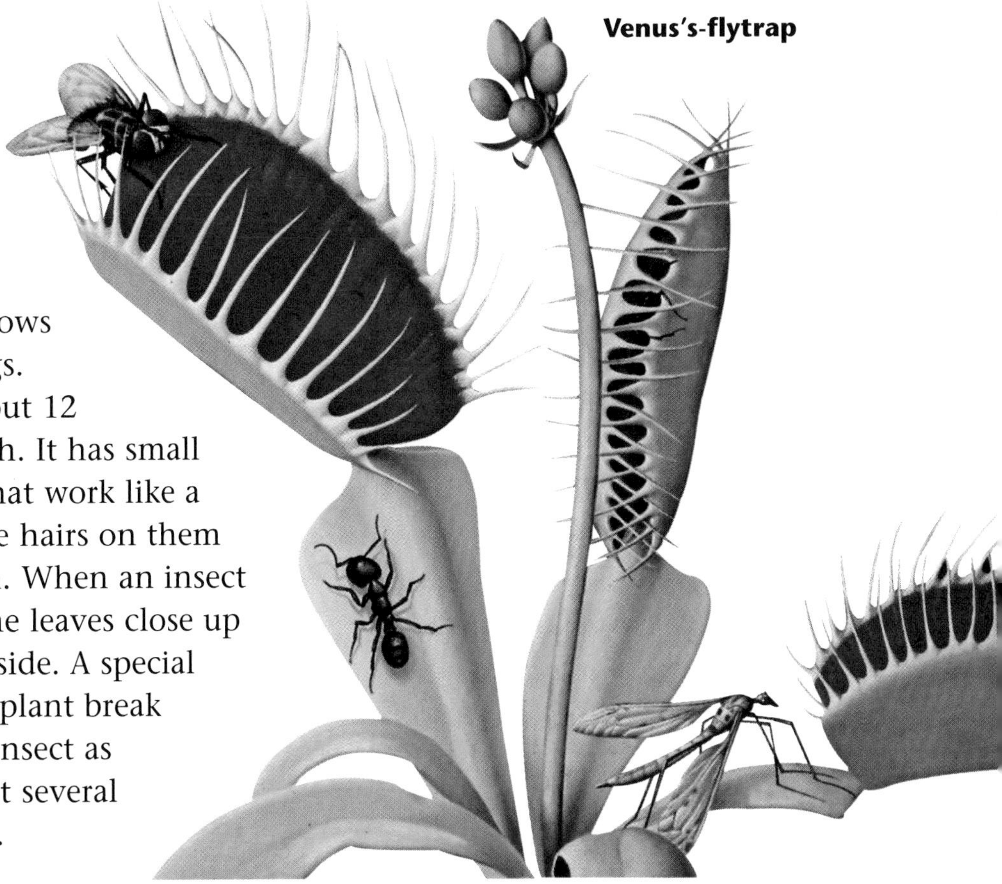

Venus's-flytrap

Vermont (blue) ranks 43rd in size among the states.

State flag

State seal

Vermont

Vermont is one of the six New England states of the United States. It lies along the Canada border between New York and New Hampshire. Massachusetts lies to the south. Vermont is called the *Green Mountain State* for the Green Mountains that stretch down the middle.

Montpelier is the capital of Vermont. It lies along the Winooski River in the north-central part of the state. Burlington is Vermont's largest city. It stands on the east shore of Lake Champlain in northwestern Vermont. Rutland is the second largest city.

Autumn in White River Junction, Vermont

Land. Vermont is known for its beautiful mountains, lakes, and forests.

The Connecticut River Valley lies along Vermont's eastern border. This area slowly turns into rugged hills toward the middle of the state.

The Champlain Valley in western Vermont spreads out around Lake Champlain. A series of islands in Lake Champlain is part of Vermont.

The Taconic Mountains in southwestern Vermont have many swift-flowing streams, thick green forests, and clear blue lakes.

Resources and products. Many of Vermont's industries use its forest and mineral resources. Trees are used for making paper, furniture, and many other wood products. Maple syrup comes from the sugar maple trees that grow there. Vermont's factories produce more maple syrup than any other state. Vermont granite and marble are used in buildings and memorials, and slate is used for roofing.

Vermont does not have much good farmland. Most farms raise dairy cows and beef cattle. Hay, oats, and corn are grown as animal feed. Potatoes, apples, flowers, and garden plants are found in the Champlain Valley and the Connecticut River Valley.

Important dates in Vermont

Indian days	Vermont was mainly an Indian hunting ground before European settlers came. The Abenaki, Mahican, and Penacook tribes were among the groups from that region.
1609	French explorer Samuel de Champlain traveled in the Vermont region. He claimed the area for France.
1724	Massachusetts established Fort Dummer, the first permanent white settlement in the Vermont region.
1763	England gained control of Vermont.
1770	Vermont settlers established a military force called the Green Mountain Boys to defend their land.
1775	Ethan Allen, Benedict Arnold, and other Green Mountain Boys captured Fort Ticonderoga from the British in the Revolutionary War.
1791	Vermont became the 14th U.S. state on March 4.
1823	The opening of the Champlain Canal created a water route from Vermont to New York City. The canal allowed Vermont farmers to ship their goods to New York.
1881	Chester A. Arthur, born in Fairfield, became the 21st president of the United States.
1923	Calvin Coolidge, born in Plymouth Notch, became the 30th President of the United States.
1970	The Vermont legislature passed the Environmental Control Law. This law allowed Vermont to limit major developments that could harm the state's environment.
1984	Madeleine M. Kunin became the first woman to be elected governor of Vermont.

The Green Mountain Boys, led by Ethan Allen, captured Fort Ticonderoga from the British in 1775.

English and French armies around Lake Champlain fought during the French and Indian War (1754-1763).

Other articles to read: **Allen, Ethan; Arthur, Chester A.; Champlain, Samuel de; Coolidge, Calvin.**

Facts About Vermont

Capital: Montpelier.

Area: 9,615 sq. mi. (24,903 km^2).

Population: 608,827.

Year of statehood: 1791.

State abbreviations: Vt. (traditional), VT (postal).

State motto: Freedom and Unity.

State song: "Hail, Vermont!" Words and music by Josephine Hovey Perry.

Largest cities: Burlington, Essex, Rutland.

Government:

State government:

Governor: 2-year term.
State senators: 30; 2-year terms.
State representatives: 150; 2-year terms.
Towns: 237 (towns, rather than counties, are the main units of local government in Vermont).

Federal government:

U.S. senators: 2
U.S. representatives: 1
Electoral votes: 3

State bird
Hermit thrush

State flower
Red clover

Versailles, Palace of

The Hall of Mirrors is one of the most famous rooms in the Palace of Versailles.

The Palace of Versailles (*vehr SY*) is a large, fancy palace in northern France. It was built by King Louis XIV in the 1600's. The palace stands about 11 miles (18 kilometers) southwest of Paris. The palace was the home of royal families of France for more than 100 years. It is now a national museum. People from all over the world go to Versailles to visit the palace and its beautiful gardens.

The palace is more than $\frac{1}{4}$ mile (0.4 kilometer) long and has about 1,300 rooms. One of the most famous rooms in the palace is called the Hall of Mirrors. It is a long hallway lined with mirrors. The palace also has paintings and sculptures by famous European artists.

Vertebrate

A vertebrate (*VUR tuh briht*) is an animal with a backbone. Animals without backbones are called invertebrates (*ihn VUR tuh brihts*).

Vertebrates are animals with backbones. All mammals, such as the polar bear, are vertebrates.

The backbone is the part of the skeleton that runs down the center of the back. It is also called the spine. The backbone of most vertebrates is made of several small bones called vertebrae (*VUR tuh BREE*). The backbone helps animals stand, sit up, and move around. It also protects the spinal cord. The spinal cord is part of the animal's nervous system, along with the brain and the nerves.

All birds, such as this great blue heron, are vertebrates. Like mammals, they have backbones.

There are about 40,000 kinds of vertebrates. Birds, fish, lizards, frogs, and salamanders are vertebrates. So are cats, dogs, bears, human beings, and all other mammals. Most animals on the earth are invertebrates, however. There are more than 1 million known kinds of invertebrates. They include clams, insects, jellyfish, sea urchins, snails, spiders, sponges, and worms.

All vertebrates have some features in common. In all vertebrates, the left and right sides of the body are alike. The body of a vertebrate typically has a head and a trunk. The trunk is the main part of the body. Some vertebrates have a neck. Vertebrates never have more than two pairs of limbs. The limbs may be legs, arms, or wings. Vertebrates also have an advanced brain covered by a bony skull.

Vertebrates were the last big group of animals to develop on the earth millions of years ago. The first vertebrates were fish without jaws or teeth. They sucked tiny pieces of food from the ocean floor. Fish developed jaws and teeth about 420 million years ago. Fish with jaws could catch and eat larger animals. The Age of Fishes began about 410 million years ago. One group of fish during this period developed thick, rounded fins. These fish may have climbed up on land on their thick fins to become land vertebrates.

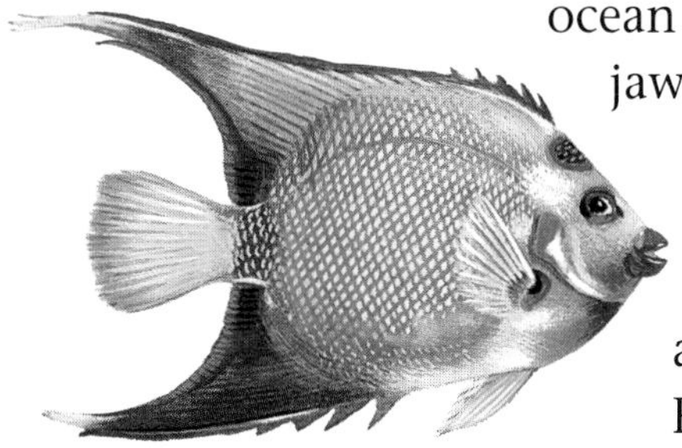

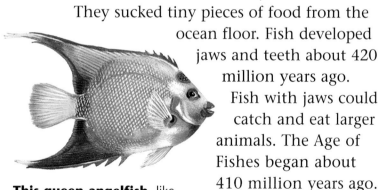

This queen angelfish, like all other fish, is a vertebrate. It has a backbone.

Other articles to read: **Amphibian; Bird; Fish; Invertebrate; Mammal; Prehistoric animal.**

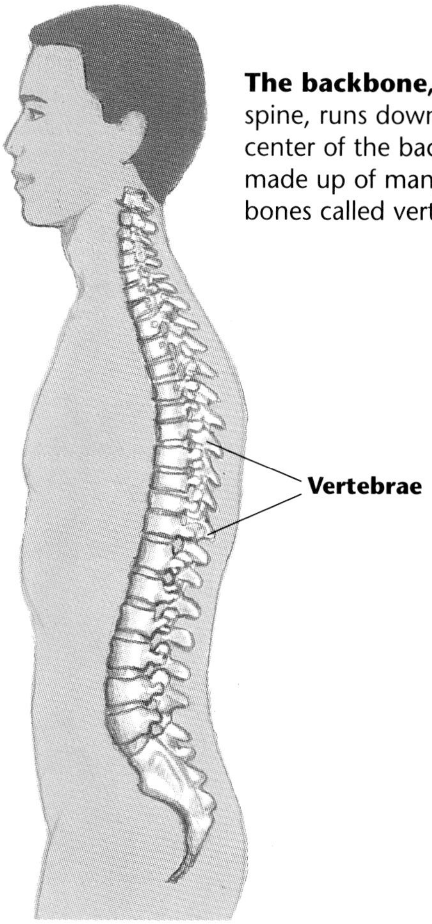

The backbone, or spine, runs down the center of the back. It is made up of many small bones called vertebrae.

Amerigo Vespucci

Vespucci, Amerigo

Amerigo Vespucci (*uh MEHR uh GOH veh SPOO chee*) (1454-1512) was an Italian explorer. America was named after him.

In the late 1490's and early 1500's, Vespucci made voyages to the eastern coast of South America. A German mapmaker thought Vespucci was the first person to reach the "New World." However, we know Christopher Columbus was the first explorer to reach this area. He arrived in 1492.

In 1507, the German mapmaker wrote "America" on a map of what is now South America. He used the word *America* to honor Vespucci. The word *America* is a form of the name *Amerigo*. Soon, this name was used throughout Europe. It was later also used for North America.

Vesuvius

Vesuvius (*vuh SOO vee uhs*) is an active volcano in Europe. An active volcano may erupt, or explode, at any time. Vesuvius rises about 7 miles (11 kilometers) southeast of the city of Naples, Italy.

Vesuvius erupts often. However, many people still live on the mountain and in the region around it. This area has rich soil and is famous for growing good wine grapes.

The first recorded eruption of Mount Vesuvius took place about 2,000 years ago. The volcano covered the cities of Herculaneum (*hur kyuh LAY nee uhm*) and Pompeii (*pahm PAY*) with ashes and lava. Thousands of people were killed. The cities remained buried until the 1700's, when people in Italy began to uncover them. Scientists now closely watch the volcano.

Other articles to read: **Pompeii.**

Mount Vesuvius is shown erupting in this photo of Naples, Italy, taken more than 100 years ago. The volcano still gives off steam, cinders, and sometimes lava.

Victoria

Victoria (1819-1901) was queen of the United Kingdom of Great Britain and Ireland. She ruled from 1837 to 1901. The time of Victoria's rule is often called the Victorian Age.

Victoria was only 18 years old when she became queen, but she is one of the most famous rulers in her country's history. She ruled the United Kingdom longer than any other king or queen in British history. The United Kingdom reached the height of its power during Victoria's rule. It expanded its empire into many countries and built many businesses and factories at home.

Victoria became queen after her uncle, King William IV, died in 1837. She was crowned on June 28, 1838. Victoria married a cousin, Prince Albert, in 1840. The couple had four sons and five daughters. When Victoria died, her eldest son became King Edward VII.

Queen Victoria

Video game

Handheld video games are small and operate with batteries.

A video game is an electronic game. It is played on a screen, such as a television screen or a computer monitor. Most video games have sound, pictures, and movies. They come in different sizes. The smallest are handheld, battery-operated toys. Many of the largest video games stand on the floor in game rooms called arcades.

Many video games involve exciting stories. Other video games are based on sports, card games, word games, or board games, such as chess. Some games have characters and stories from popular movies. A number of video games help players learn to spell or count. Some games test how fast a player can respond to action.

To play a video game, players operate controls that move dots, lines, or other pictures that appear on the screen. Most games are controlled through a lever called a joystick. Other games use special control pads or computer keyboards. Some games are controlled by spoken commands.

Many video games are played on special machines at home. Some machines must be connected to a television set or a computer. Other games can be played on the computer itself. A video game can come on a video cartridge or a round electronic computer disc called a CD-ROM. Video games were first developed in the early 1970's. The first successful arcade video game appeared in 1972. It was called Pong.

Some video games are large machines. People go to game rooms called arcades to play them.

Videotape recorder

Videotape recordings of pictures and sounds can be played on television sets with VCR's.

A videotape recorder is a machine that records pictures and sound. It is also known as a VTR or video recorder. Videotape recordings are made on special magnetic tape called videotape. This tape can be played on TV sets with machines called video players, also commonly known as VCR's (videocassette recorders).

People use VTR's in many ways. Television producers use videotape recordings in commercials, TV shows, and news programs. Many schools and businesses use VTR's to record educational programs, and employee-training films. People use VCR's at home to record favorite TV programs and to play recordings of movies, concerts, and other events.

Some videotape recorders are used to make home movies. These machines are called camcorders. They have both a camera and a recorder. Camcorders run on batteries.

Most recorders use tape cassettes. The tape is a long plastic strip coated with a thin layer of material called iron oxide. This material holds pictures and sounds in special magnetic patterns. VTR's record television programs by changing the pictures and sounds into magnetic patterns. These patterns are recorded on the tape. When the tape is played, the VTR changes the magnetic patterns back into pictures and sounds.

Other articles to read: **Television.**

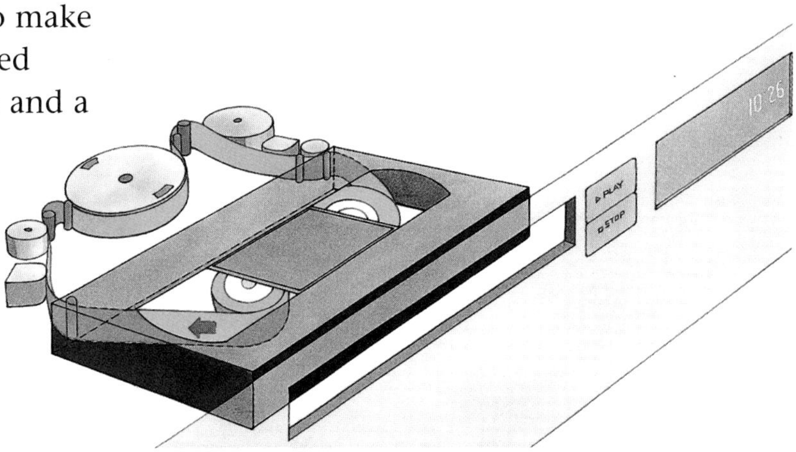

Special tape made of plastic and tiny pieces of metal is used by videocassette recorders to store pictures and sounds.

Vienna

Vienna (*vee EHN uh*) is the capital and largest city of Austria. It lies in northeastern Austria on the Danube River. Vienna is the center of Austria's arts, business, and government.

A historical area of the city called the Inner City stands in the middle of Vienna. A band of streets called the Ringstrassen encircles this area. Some of Vienna's most beautiful buildings are along these streets.

During the 1700's and 1800's, Vienna was a world center of education, literature, music, and science. From 1867 to 1918, it was the capital city of Austria-Hungary, a country in central Europe. When Austria-Hungary collapsed after World War I ended in 1918, Vienna lost much of its importance.

Vienna is famous for its art galleries, churches, and theaters. The Burgtheater, *above,* is an important theater that is supported by the Austrian government.

The old Inner City of Vienna has many sidewalk cafes and beautiful buildings.

Vietnam

Vietnam (*VEE eht NAHM*) is a tropical country in Southeast Asia. It extends south from China in a long, thin S-shape. Vietnam shares borders with Laos and Cambodia on the west. The South China Sea lies to the east. Hanoi (*hah NOY*) is the capital of Vietnam, and Ho Chi Minh (*hoh chee mihn*) City is the largest city.

Vietnam is run by a Communist government. Communism is a system in which the government owns the businesses, factories, and farms, and everything is supposed to be shared by all the people.

Land. Mountains stretch across much of Vietnam. Forests or jungles cover most of the mountains. The southernmost part of Vietnam is mostly flat. It is the chief farming area of Vietnam. Rice is raised throughout the lowlands along the South China Sea.

People. Thousands of years ago, people moved into what is now Vietnam from the north and from islands to the south. Most of the Vietnamese people probably came from these two groups. Today, Vietnamese people make up most of the country's population. Other groups include the Chinese, Thai, and Khmer—one of the oldest groups in Southeast Asia. Vietnamese is the official language.

Most of Vietnam's people live in the countryside. In the north, many people build wood or bamboo houses with tiled roofs. In the south, most houses have walls made of palm leaves or straw and roofs of straw, metal, or plastic. The people wear mostly cotton clothing. Most of the people eat mainly rice, fish, and vegetables.

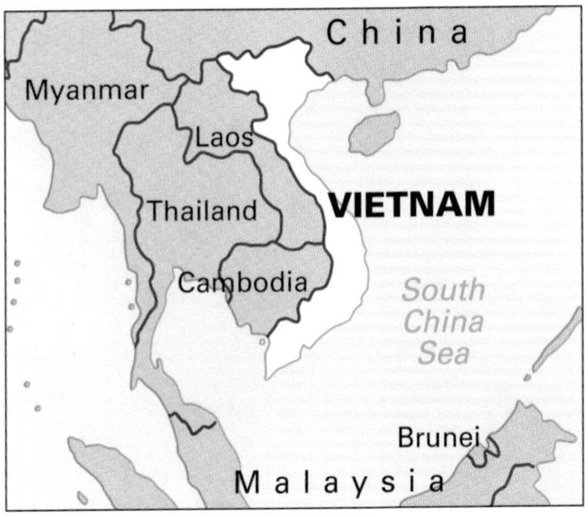

Vietnam and its neighbors

Facts About Vietnam

Capital: Hanoi.

Area: 128,066 sq. mi. (331,689 km²).

Population: Estimated 2006 population—84,655,000.

Official language: Vietnamese.

Climate: Hot, with rainy storms called monsoons throughout the year. Most of Vietnam has two seasons—a wet, hot summer and a drier, slightly cooler winter.

Chief products:

Agriculture: rice.

Manufacturing: cement, fertilizer, iron and steel, paper products, shoes, steel, textiles.

Mining: coal.

Form of government: Communist state.

Flag

Resources and products. Vietnam gets most of its money from farming. More than half of the workers are farmers. Rice is the chief farm product of Vietnam. The fishing industry is also important in Vietnam. Thousands of people who live along the coast fish for a living. They catch lobster, shrimp, squid, and many kinds of fish. The nation's natural resources include coal, oil, and wood from the forests.

History. Thousands of years ago, the Vietnamese people lived in what is now northern Vietnam. China ruled the area for about 1,000 years. In 939, the Vietnamese formed an independent state. Over the centuries, they slowly increased its size.

France took control of Vietnam in the 1800's. During World War II (1939-1945), Japan moved in. After Japan lost the war in 1945, France tried to take back control of Vietnam. But fighting broke out in 1946 between French forces and a Vietnamese Communist group called the Vietminh (*VEE eht MIHN*). In 1954, as part of a peace settlement, Vietnam was divided into North Vietnam and South Vietnam. The Communists got control of North Vietnam. Non-Communist Vietnamese leaders got control of South Vietnam.

Many people in Vietnam earn their living by fishing. These fishing boats are in Halong Bay, the Gulf of Tonkin, Vietnam.

In 1957, Vietminh people who lived in the South began to fight against the South Vietnamese government. These Vietminh became known as the Viet Cong. North Vietnam began supporting the Viet Cong in 1959. The Communists wanted to control the whole country. The fighting developed into the Vietnam War (1957-1975). In April 1975, the Communists won out over the forces in South Vietnam and took control of it. In 1976, they created a single nation, which the Communists named the Socialist Republic of Vietnam.

Other articles to read: **Vietnam War.**

Vietnam War

The Vietnam War was fought over the control of Vietnam. It began in 1957 and ended in 1975. Communists fought on one side, and non-Communists fought on the other.

The war began when Communist fighters called the Viet Cong tried to take over South Vietnam. At that time, Vietnam was divided into North and South Vietnam. North Vietnam was Communist, and South Vietnam was not. Communism is a system in which everything is owned by the government and is supposed to be shared equally by the people.

The United States feared that if one Southeast Asian nation became Communist, other countries in Southeast Asia would also become Communist. So the United States sent equipment and soldiers to help South Vietnam fight the Viet Cong.

North Vietnam supported the Viet Cong. It wanted to make the north and south into one Communist nation. China and the Soviet Union gave the Vietnamese Communists materials to help them fight the war. At that time, China and the Soviet Union were the world's largest Communist nations.

Hanoi was the capital of North Vietnam during the Vietnam War. Today, the city is the capital of the united Vietnam.

The United States and other nations sent troops to help the South Vietnamese but could not defeat the Viet Cong. After years of fighting and thousands of deaths, the Vietnam War seemed endless. In 1973, the United States stopped fighting the war and sent its soldiers home. The war ended when South Vietnam surrendered, or gave up, to North Vietnam on April 30, 1975. In 1976, Vietnam became a single nation.

Other articles to read: **Communism.**

Vikings

This gold bracelet was made by Vikings.

The Vikings were a group of pirates and warriors. They lived in Scandinavia, a part of Europe that includes what are now Denmark, Norway, and Sweden. From the late 700's to about 1100, Viking sailors spread great fear through western Europe. They burned and stole things in towns on coasts and along rivers. But they also explored parts of the world that were unknown to other Europeans. Bold Viking sailors explored the North Atlantic Ocean and even reached America.

Viking life

Most Vikings worked as farmers. Many also hunted and fished. Some Vikings made metal objects, built ships, or carved wood. Some traveled far to buy and sell goods.

The Vikings lived in villages. Their houses had walls made of wood or stone and a roof covered with shingles, straw, or packed soil called sod. Each home included a place for fires called a hearth. The hearth provided heat and light as well as a place to cook. Viking houses had no windows.

The Vikings spoke a language related to German. They used an alphabet made up of characters called runes (*roonz*).

Religion played an important role in the Viking way of life. The Vikings worshiped a number of gods. They believed that if they died fighting, they would go to a great hall called Valhalla in the home of the gods. There, they could fight all day and eat all night.

The three most important gods were Odin, Thor, and Frey. Odin was the king of all the gods and goddesses. Thor was the god of lightning, thunder, rain, storms, and winds. He was the most popular god because his power over the weather

Vikings were skilled at building ships and finding their way across oceans. Some reached lands that are now part of North America.

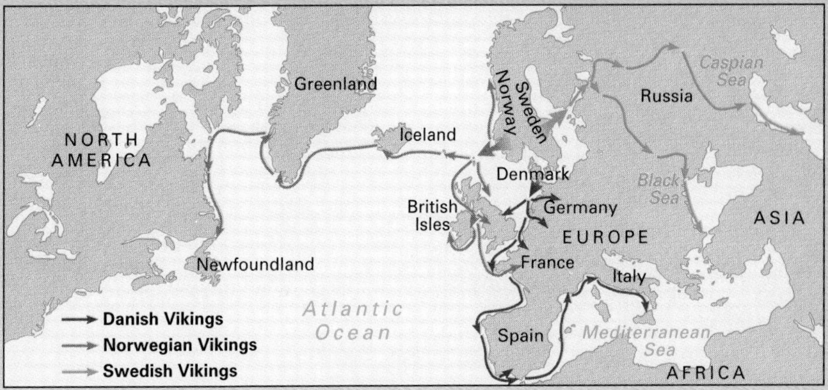

Lands explored by the Vikings

had a great effect on the lives of the people. The Vikings prayed to Thor for good harvests and good luck. Frey was the god of farming and love.

The Vikings had special ways of burying the dead. Many rich Viking men and women who died were laid in a ship that was then buried. The Vikings believed that ship graves provided a safe and comfortable journey to the land of the dead. Beds, jewelry, weapons, and other belongings were also placed in the ship. In some cases, the dead person's dogs and slaves were buried alive in a ship grave.

Shipbuilding and sailing

The Vikings were among the best shipbuilders of their time. They built both trading ships and warships. Viking shipbuilders greatly improved the sailing ability of Scandinavian ships by adding

Most Vikings lived in small farming communities, built near a river or inlet to the sea.

Fierce Viking raiders were feared all over Europe by people who lived near rivers or the sea. The Vikings' swift warships allowed them to make surprise attacks, then quickly escape.

a keel. A keel is a long, narrow piece of wood attached to the underside of a ship. It makes a ship steadier and easier to steer. The keel made Viking ships faster than before.

A Viking warship traveled well in either rough seas or calm waters. At sea, the warships used winds and sails for power. On a river, the warships became giant rowboats. A warship had from 15 to more than 30 pairs of oars. The front end of a Viking warship curved upward and had a woodcarving of the head of a dragon or snake.

To find their way at sea, the Vikings used the sun, the stars, and landmarks. The position of the sun and stars helped them figure out their directions at sea. Landmarks told them where they were. They later developed simple tools to help them sail. Sometimes, Viking sailors used birds called ravens to help them. These birds were known for being able to find land. The Vikings would set loose a raven from the ship and then sail in the same direction that the bird flew. The raven became a favorite symbol of the Vikings. It was shown on their flag.

Wars and attacks

Viking sailors were cruel, and other Europeans greatly feared them. Some people thought the Vikings were crazy. Viking sailors burned villages, killed men, women, and children, and sailed away with slaves and treasure. They became known for surprise attacks. They often struck so fast that people had no chance to defend themselves.

For many years, the Vikings traveled on ships, fighting wars and attacking villages to get cattle and horses, food, and valuable objects made of gold or silver. Sometimes, Vikings arrived with several hundred warships and thousands of warriors. But most attacks were made by small groups of men in just a few ships. Vikings usually attacked small towns, farms, churches, and monasteries, or places where holy men called monks lived.

The warriors fought mainly with axes, bows and arrows, spears, and swords. Most Vikings carried round wooden shields for protection. Many wore armor made from thick layers of animal skins. Only Viking leaders wore helmets and coats of metal armor. Pictures often show Viking warriors wearing helmets with cattle horns on the sides, but the Vikings never had such helmets.

Viking craftworkers made this brooch of gold, silver, and bronze.

Exploration and trade

Vikings were important explorers. Viking ships carried settlers to Iceland, and later to Greenland, which was unknown to Europeans at that time. Leif Ericson, a Viking explorer, landed in North America about 500 years before Christopher Columbus arrived there in 1492. The Vikings established a settlement in North America, but it lasted only a few years.

The Vikings robbed and burned parts of England, France, Germany, Ireland, Italy, Russia, and Spain. At first, they attacked these areas just to rob them. Many Vikings saw attacking and robbing as a way to get rich and be honored by the community. Later, the Vikings set up businesses for selling and buying goods in other countries. They sailed to most parts of the known world and traded farm products, furs, and slaves for gold, silk, silver, and weapons.

Village

A village is made up of a small group of houses. It is usually smaller than a town. The business center and the social center of a town are sometimes called the village. When people talk about government, the word *village* means a community with a small government that takes care of the community's business. This small government may include a village president and a group of people called a board of trustees. A village government also has other workers, including police officers.

The village of Ile d'Orleans, Quebec, Canada

Each part of a village government has some responsibility for the well-being of its people. It also provides certain services. People who live in the village pay taxes for some of these services.

Villages were set up by prehistoric people thousands of years ago. These prehistoric villages had simple rules. Most villages had a few leaders who made decisions for the village and workers who did certain jobs in the village. As the communities grew, these leaders and workers handled more community business and provided more services for the people. Today, village workers include mayors, garbage collectors, police officers, and teachers.

After people discovered how to farm about 11,000 years ago, they began to gather in one place to tend their crops. These early settlements became the first villages.

Virgin Islands (United Kingdom)

The Virgin Islands are a group of small islands between the Caribbean Sea and the Atlantic Ocean. Some islands belong to the United States, and some belong to the United Kingdom. The islands of the United Kingdom are called the British Virgin Islands. They include Anegada (*AN uh GAH duh*), Jost van Dyke (*YOHST van DYK*), Tortola, the Virgin Gorda islands, and other islands nearby.

There are more than 60 islands in the British Virgin Islands. They have a land area of 59 square miles (153 square kilometers). Vacationers go there to enjoy the beautiful weather and beaches.

The Italian explorer Christopher Columbus came to the islands in 1493. The British have controlled the islands since 1672.

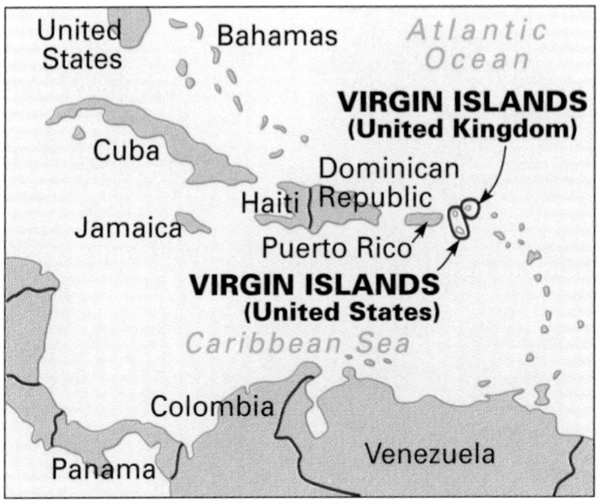

The Virgin Islands and its neighbors

Virgin Islands (United States)

The Virgin Islands are a group of small islands between the Caribbean Sea and the Atlantic Ocean. Some islands belong to the United States, and some belong to the United Kingdom. The United States islands include St. Croix (*saynt kroy*), St. John, St. Thomas, and other islands nearby.

The U.S. Virgin Islands cover 132 square miles (342 square kilometers). The islands are known for their beauty and warm weather. Many people visit to enjoy the beaches and the fishing.

The Italian explorer Christopher Columbus came to the Virgin Islands in 1493. Denmark started a settlement on St. Thomas. Denmark got control of St. John and St. Croix in the 1700's. In 1917, Denmark sold these islands to the United States.

Charlotte Amalie on the island of St. Thomas is the capital of the United States Virgin Islands.

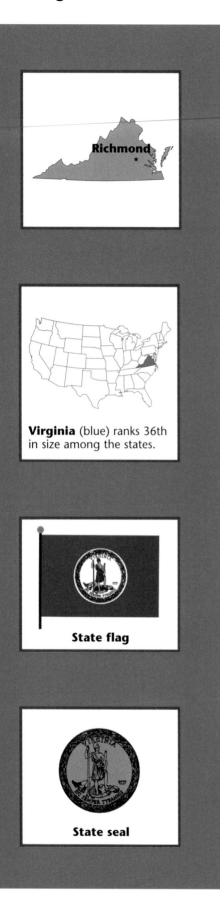

Virginia (blue) ranks 36th in size among the states.

State flag

State seal

Virginia

Virginia is one of the southern states of the United States. It lies along the Atlantic Ocean. Maryland, West Virginia, and Kentucky lie to the north and west, and North Carolina and Tennessee lie to the south. Virginia is also called the *Old Dominion.* King Charles II gave Virginia that name when it was an English colony.

Richmond is the capital of Virginia. It lies in east-central Virginia. It has many old homes and churches.

Virginia Beach is the state's largest city. It lies where Chesapeake Bay meets the Atlantic Ocean.

Shenandoah National Park, Virginia

Land. Virginia is a beautiful land of mountains, rivers, plains, and valleys. Along the Atlantic coastline, sand bars and small islands have made shallow lakes called lagoons. A lowland spreads out across eastern Virginia. The middle of the state is plains.

Western Virginia has many mountains and valleys. The forest-covered Blue Ridge Mountains are the highest. The Shenandoah Valley is a beautiful area of hilly plains.

Resources and products. Virginia is an important state for trade and industry. Chemicals are the state's leading product. Tobacco products, food products, boats, ships, car parts, and trucks are also made in Virginia.

Farming and fishing are major industries, too. Farmers raise chickens, turkeys, hogs, and beef cattle. Tobacco, corn, hay, peanuts, and soybeans are the chief crops. Farmers near Chesapeake Bay grow vegetables. Fishing fleets catch a variety of seafood.

Virginia is a leading coal-mining state. Other mineral products include crushed stone, limestone, and granite.

Important dates in Virginia

Indian days	Many Native American peoples lived in the Virginia region before Europeans arrived. They included the Cherokee, Monacan, and Powhatan tribes.
1607	The Virginia Company of London started Jamestown, the first permanent European settlement in Virginia.
1624	Virginia became a royal colony of England.
1775	Virginia's George Washington became commander of the army in the Revolutionary War.
1776	Virginia declared its independence and adopted its first constitution. Thomas Jefferson of Virginia wrote the Declaration of Independence.
1788	Virginia became the 10th U.S. state on June 25.
1789	George Washington became the first U.S. president.
1801-1825	Three Virginians in a row were president: Thomas Jefferson (1801-1809), James Madison (1809-1817), and James Monroe (1817-1825).
1831	Nat Turner led a famous slave revolt.
1841	William Henry Harrison, born in Virginia, became president. Harrison died a month later. Vice President John Tyler, also a Virginian, became president.
1849	Zachary Taylor, another Virginian, became president.
1861-1865	Virginia seceded from, or left, the United States and fought against the United States in the Civil War.
1869	Virginia adopted a new state constitution that made slavery against the law and gave black Virginian men the right to vote.
1870	Virginia became a U.S. state again.
1912	Woodrow Wilson became the eighth Virginian to be elected U.S. president.
1959	Public schools in Arlington County and Norfolk became the first in Virginia to accept both black and white children.
1989	L. Douglas Wilder of Virginia was the first African American to be elected governor of a U.S. state.

Jamestown was the first permanent English settlement in America. Captain John Smith and a group of English colonists established the settlement in May 1607.

Other articles to read: **Civil War; Colonies, Thirteen; Harrison, William Henry; Jefferson, Thomas; Madison, James; Monroe, James; Revolutionary War in America; Taylor, Zachary; Tyler, John; Washington, George; Wilson, Woodrow.**

Facts About Virginia

Capital: Richmond.

Area: 40,598 sq. mi. (105,149 km²).

Population: 7,078,515.

Year of statehood: 1788.

State abbreviations: Va. (traditional), VA (postal).

State motto: *Sic Semper Tyrannis* (Thus Always to Tyrants).

State song: none. Virginia gave up its old state song in 1997. It does not yet have a new one.

Largest cities: Virginia Beach, Norfolk, Chesapeake.

Government:

State government:

Governor: 4-year term.
State senators: 40; 4-year terms.
State representatives: 100; 2-year terms.
Counties: 95.

Federal government:

U.S. senators: 2.
U.S. representatives: 11.
Electoral votes: 13.

State bird
Cardinal

State flower
Flowering dogwood

Virtual reality

Virtual reality (VR) is a three-dimensional electronic environment created by a computer and other equipment. When people use this equipment, they feel as if they are in a world created by the computer. In this world, they can look at and seem to handle objects as if they were really there. VR systems are widely used in video games. They are also used to help train athletes, pilots, and others.

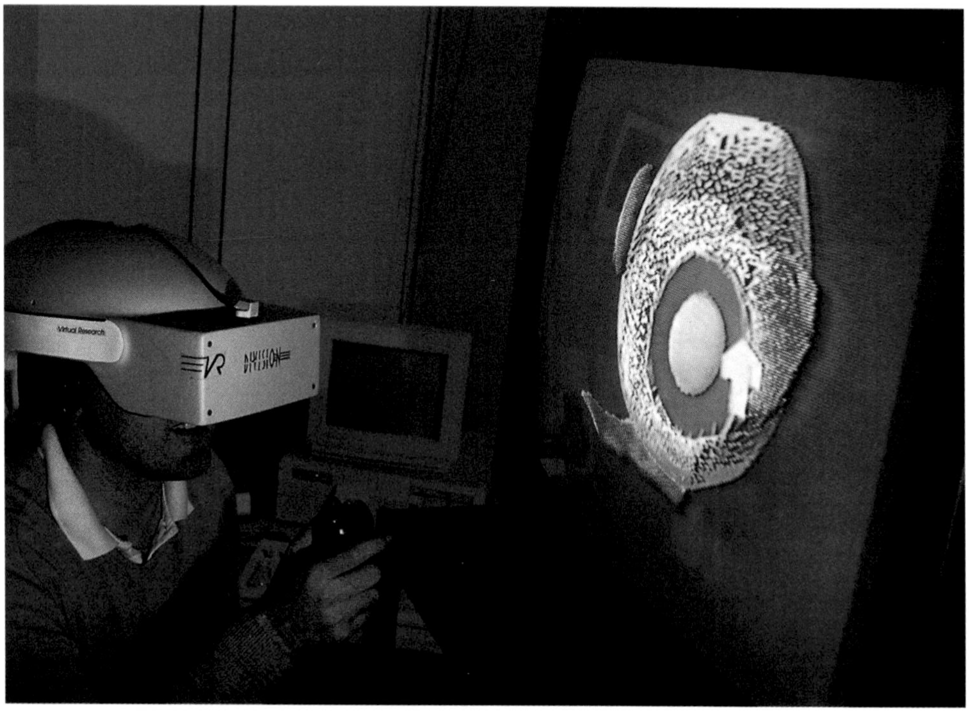

Surgeons use virtual reality (VR) to practice operating on eyes, and to teach students how to do so. VR allows doctors and students to watch the operation from any point of view, something that is not possible when operating on a real patient.

Most VR systems have a special headset. The headset has two small TV screens, one for each eye. The headset is connected to a computer. The screens show electronic pictures. The pictures for each eye are slightly different in a way that makes objects look as if they could be picked up. Some headsets have a small speaker for each ear. The system's computer sends sound into these speakers. The sound helps make what the user sees seem real.

Another common VR tool is a special glove that senses movements of the user's hand. This glove is also connected to the computer. A picture of the glove appears on the headset screens. As the user's hand moves, the computer makes the pictures of the glove move in the same way. This system makes users feel that they can grab objects in the electronic world. Other equipment makes users feel as if the objects have weight. It can also make the users feel as if they could move around in the electronic world.

Research on equipment that developed into VR began in the early 1960's. When inexpensive flat TV screens became available in the late 1980's, a few companies began to sell special VR headsets. VR games appeared in stores and video game rooms in the early 1990's. Today's virtual reality systems do not have quite the appearance of real-world objects and situations, but they are good enough for video games. Researchers are working to improve them.

Virus

A virus is a tiny thing that attacks the cells of plants, animals, and bacteria. Viruses are shaped like needles or like balls. Most viruses can be seen only with a powerful microscope. Viruses are sometimes called germs (*juhrmz*).

Viruses cause many diseases. Virus diseases in human beings include AIDS, chickenpox, colds, cold sores, flu, measles, mumps, and rabies. Viruses also cause disease and cancer in animals and damage food crops. Some virus diseases can spread from one kind of animal to another kind of animal. A few animal viruses can make human

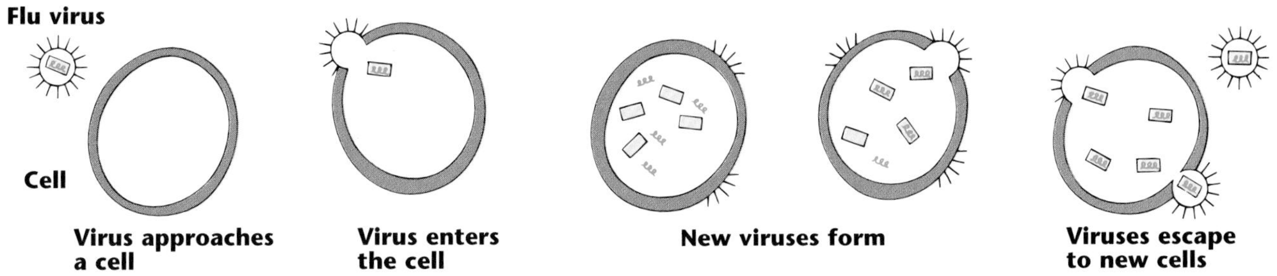

After a flu virus infects a cell, *above,* new viruses quickly form inside the cell. The new viruses escape to infect other cells. As cell after cell is quickly infected, the person falls ill.

beings sick. For example, the rabies virus harms both dogs and people.

By itself, a virus is a lifeless thing. However, inside a living body, a virus can make more of itself. A virus can get into a human body in several ways. A virus may get into a person's blood through a cut, or a person may breathe in a virus through the air. A person may also eat or drink something that contains a virus. Once inside the body, the virus moves through the blood or other fluids to certain cells (*sehlz*). Cells are the building blocks of all living things. Inside the cells, the virus gets busy. It uses the materials inside the cell to live, and it starts to make copies of itself. These

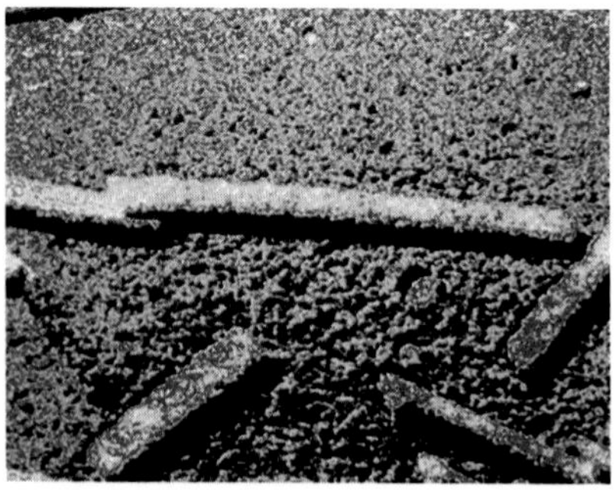

Rod-shaped tobacco virus

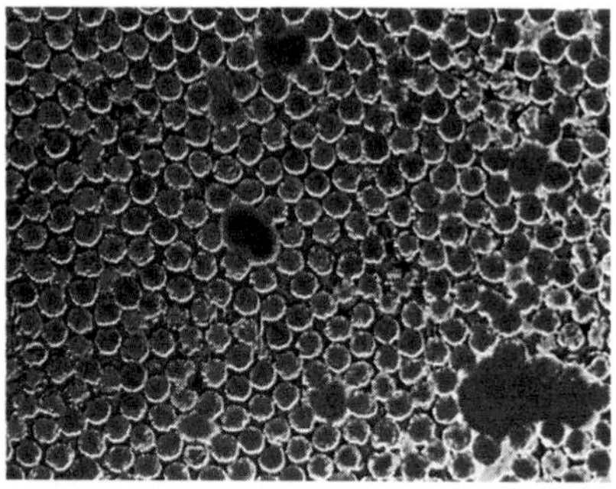

Sphere-shaped polio virus

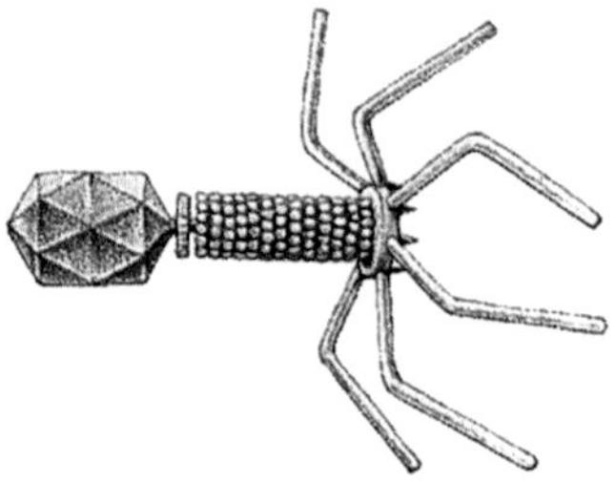

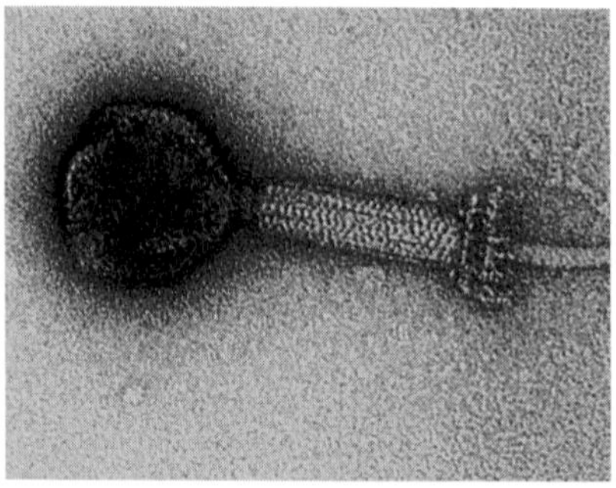

Bacteriophage

Viruses
Some, such as tobacco viruses, look like rods. Others, such as polio viruses, look like spheres. A third kind, the bacteriophage, is a virus with a tail.

virus copies spread to other cells. They cause disease by killing or damaging cells.

Doctors cannot kill viruses with drugs because most drugs that can kill a virus would also kill healthy cells in the person's body. So people protect themselves from diseases caused by viruses by getting special shots called vaccines (*vak SEENZ*). Vaccines cause the body to produce cells that help fight viruses when they show up.

Insects carry plant viruses. When insects eat plants, the viruses get into the plant cells. Viruses attack tiny living things called bacteria, too. Viruses have special parts like needles that poke a hole in bacteria walls and get into the cells.

Other articles to read: **AIDS; Chickenpox; Cold, common; Immunization; Influenza; Inoculation; Measles; Mumps; Pneumonia; Rubella; Salk, Jonas Edward.**

Virus, computer

A computer virus is a computer program that sometimes damages the information stored on computers. It also attacks the software used by a computer. Software is computer programming that tells the computer how to do certain things.

A computer virus can delete, change, or add information. It can get into computers from storage devices, such as CD-ROM's, or from modems. A modem is a machine computers use to send and receive information across telephone lines. A computer hooks up to the Internet through a modem. If a computer is hooked up to other computers, the virus can make copies of itself and get into the other computers. Today, people use special antivirus programs to prevent viruses from getting into their computers.

A computer virus can delete, change, or add information.

Vitamin

A vitamin is a material found in foods that makes the body grow and stay healthy. There are 13 vitamins. They are vitamins A, C, D, E, K, and a group of 8 B vitamins. Each vitamin does things for the body that no other vitamin can do. For example, vitamin A is necessary for healthy skin and bones. It is found in liver, eggs, and milk. Vitamin C is needed for the ligaments, which hold the bones together, as well as for healing cuts. It is found in fruits and potatoes. Vitamin D prevents rickets, a disease that harms bones. It is often added to milk. Vitamin E helps the body's cells stay healthy. It is found in vegetable oils and whole-grain cereals. Vitamin K helps make blood thicken near a cut, so that the cut stops bleeding. Cauliflower and green leafy vegetables, such as kale and spinach, are rich in vitamin K.

The best way for a healthy person to get vitamins is by eating a balanced diet. A balanced diet includes grains, fruits, vegetables, milk or cheeses, and meats, beans, or nuts. Some people take vitamin pills every day to make sure they get enough vitamins. But too much of certain vitamins can also make a person sick.

Over time, a person who does not get enough of a certain vitamin can become ill. Scientists discovered vitamins while searching for the causes of certain illnesses.

Some important vitamins needed for good health

Vitamin	Some benefits of it	Some places it is found
A	Helps keep skin, eyes, bones, teeth, and various body systems healthy.	Carrots, dark green leafy vegetables, eggs, liver, milk, sweet potatoes, deep yellow fruits and vegetables.
B_1	Helps the heart and nervous system work properly.	Legumes, nuts, certain meats, pork, whole grains, yeast, enriched breads, and most vegetables.
B_2	Helps keep skin healthy.	Cheese, fish, green vegetables, liver, milk, poultry.
Niacin	Helps keep skin healthy.	Fish, liver, enriched breads, lean meat, whole grains.
B_6	Helps the body digest fat, protein, and carbohydrates.	Eggs, fish, nuts, certain meats, poultry, whole grains.
B_{12}	Helps the nervous system work properly.	Eggs, fish, meat, milk, poultry.
C	Needed for strong bones and teeth.	Cantaloupe, citrus fruits, potatoes, raw cabbage, strawberries, tomatoes.
D	Helps the body digest calcium and phosphorus.	Eggs, salmon, tuna, fortified milk, sunlight.
E	Helps prevent needed fatty acids in the body from burning up.	Almost all foods, but especially in margarine, olives, and vegetable oils.

Voice

A voice is a sound that comes from an animal. Almost all animals have voices. Many animals use their voices to share noise or feelings with one another. Birds make music with their voices. Dogs express their feelings with their voices. They whimper when they want something or when they feel guilty, they growl when they are angry, and they bark when they are excited or happy. Several kinds of zoo animals, such as the chimpanzee, also make sounds to show different feelings. But no animal's voice can express as much as a human being's voice.

People have created languages with their voices. These languages help people share their deepest thoughts.

In human beings, the vocal cords are the body parts that produce sound. The vocal cords are in the throat. People make sounds when air passes through the cords. Muscles stretch and relax the vocal cords. The more tightly the cords are stretched, the higher the sounds. The more relaxed the cords, the lower the sounds. This stretching and relaxing produces the different sounds in a human voice.

The length of the vocal cords also affects the sound of the voice. Women's voices are usually higher than men's because their vocal cords are shorter. The tongue, lips, teeth, and the passages in the nose also help shape the sounds of the voice.

People use their vocal cords when they speak. When people breathe in, *left,* the vocal cords are relaxed. When people speak, *right,* muscles in the larynx stretch the vocal cords tight. Air passing over them makes them vibrate and make sounds.

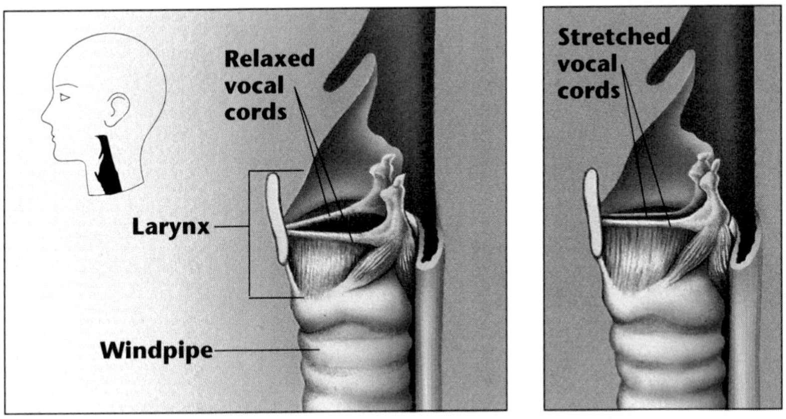

Children from many countries sing together at a festival. To hit the high notes, they stretch their vocal cords more tightly.

Steam and lava erupt from Kilauea, a volcano in Hawaii. Kilauea has erupted many times since the mid-1950's.

Volcano

A volcano is a hole or crack in the earth. Sometimes, hot rocks and gas shoot out of that crack. This blast of hot rocks and gas is called an eruption (*ih RUHP shuhn*). Most volcanoes are cone-shaped mountains.

A volcanic eruption is a breathtaking sight. In some eruptions, huge clouds of fire rise over the mountain while glowing rivers of lava flow down its sides. Lava is hot, melted rock. In other eruptions, red-hot ash shoots out of the mountaintop, and large chunks of hot rock blast high into the air. A few eruptions are so strong that they blow the mountain apart.

Most volcanoes are found along the edge of the Pacific Ocean. This area is called the Ring of Fire. Eruptions also occur in such places as Hawaii, Iceland, and southern Europe—and at the bottom of the sea.

How a volcano is formed

Powerful forces inside the earth cause volcanoes. They begin when hot melted rock called magma rises from deep within the earth. The magma is mixed with gas. The gas makes the magma lighter than the rock around it, so the magma rises through cracks in the rock. When the magma gets near the surface, the magma and gas blast out a hole called a vent. The rock and magma blown out of the vent gradually pile up around it. They form the volcanic mountain, or volcano. Once a volcano has formed, the magma sometimes escapes, or gets out, through small cracks in the sides of the volcano. Sometimes these cracks turn into small vents.

Vesuvius, a volcano near the coast of Naples, Italy, has erupted many times. The first time people wrote about the volcano erupting was in A.D. 79, when lava and ash covered three cities. This old photo shows an eruption in 1872.

A **volcano erupts** when rock deep inside the earth melts and becomes magma. Magma rises through the rock above it, and eventually blasts or melts a path to the surface. Once outside, the magma becomes lava, which flows down the slope, cools, and hardens into rock.

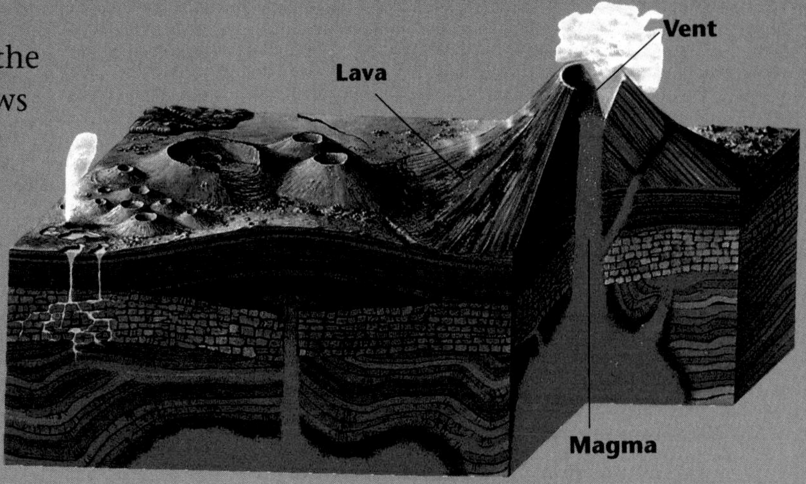

Kinds of volcanic materials

Three kinds of materials may erupt from a volcano. They are lava, chunks of rock called fragments, and gas.

Lava is magma that has burst out of the volcano. Lava is red hot. Some lava flows rapidly down a volcano's slopes. Sticky lava flows more slowly. As lava cools, it hardens. Some lava hardens into smooth, folded sheets of rock. Sticky lava cools into rough, jagged sheets of rock. The stickiest lava may form boulders or big mounds. Sometimes lava creates tunnels called lava tubes. These tubes form when the surface of flowing lava cools and hardens, but the lava underneath keeps flowing. After the flowing lava drains away, it leaves a tunnel.

Rock fragments are formed from magma that is so sticky that gas cannot easily escape from it. The trapped gas builds up within the magma and eventually blasts out, shooting pieces of magma everywhere. These pieces harden as rock fragments.

The tiniest rock fragments are called volcanic dust. The wind can blow volcanic dust all around the world. Volcanic ash is made up of larger rock fragments. It can mix with water in a stream and cause a boiling mudflow. The largest rock fragments are called volcanic bombs.

Gas pours out of volcanoes in most eruptions. This gas carries a huge amount of volcanic dust and looks like black smoke.

Hot lava flowing from Kilauea in Hawaii

A cinder cone

A composite volcano

Clouds of gas and dust pour from Surtsey, a volcanic island near Iceland.

Kinds of volcanoes

There are three main kinds of volcanoes. They are shield volcanoes, cinder cones, and composite (*kuhm PAHZ iht*) volcanoes.

Shield volcanoes are low, broad mountains. They form when lava spills from a vent and spreads widely and gradually builds up. The famous Mauna Loa (*MOW nuh LOH uh*) in Hawaii is a shield volcano.

Cinder cones are mountains shaped like cones. They form when rock fragments—especially small volcanic bombs called cinders—shoot out of a volcano and build up around the vent. Paricutín (*puh ree kuh TEEN*) in western Mexico is a well-known cinder cone. It began to form in 1943, when a crack opened in a cornfield. When the eruptions ended in 1952, the top of the cone was 1,345 feet (410 meters) high.

A shield volcano

Composite volcanoes are also shaped like cones. They form when both lava and rock fragments erupt from a volcano and pile up around the vent. Japan's beautiful Mount Fuji is a composite volcano.

Why volcanoes occur in certain places

Scientists think most volcanoes form between parts of the earth's crust called plates. Scientists believe that the earth's outer shell is made up of about 30 huge plates. The plates move slowly on a layer of magma. As they move, the plates bump into each other, spread apart, or slide past each other. Volcanoes form where magma comes up between the edges of these plates.

Other volcanoes may form where a huge tube of magma develops in the earth's rock. In some cases, the tube is close enough to the surface of the earth so that part of the magma breaks through and forms a volcano.

Predicting volcanoes

Some volcanoes are active—they erupt all the time. Others erupt only every now and then. Still others seem inactive, but scientists believe they may someday erupt. Some volcanoes are extinct (*ehk STIHNGKT*). Extinct volcanoes will probably never erupt again. Mount Kenya in Africa is an extinct volcano.

Scientists do their best to warn people when they think a volcano will erupt. Eruptions can kill people and ruin property. Sometimes small earthquakes and clouds of gas from the vent tell scientists that the volcano may be ready to explode. But most of the time, there are no signs.

Benefits of volcanoes

Volcanoes can be deadly and do great damage. However, people have found ways to use the rock and heat from volcanoes. People use volcanic rock to build roads, and farmers spread volcanic ash on soil for good plant growth. In Reykjavik, Iceland, most people heat their homes with steaming hot water piped into town from volcanic areas.

Other articles to read: **Earthquake; Kilimanjaro; Mount Fuji; Mount Saint Helens; Mountain.**

Volcanoes are helpful to people in Iceland. They drill wells like this one in volcanic areas and use the steaming hot water to heat their homes.

HANDS-ON!

Watch a Volcano

You can make a volcano that erupts with liquid and bubbly gas. Ask an adult to help you do this experiment.

Fill the cup almost full with vinegar. Add food coloring.

Fill the jar about half full with baking soda. Then wrap the cardboard around the jar to make a tube. Use tape to fasten it.

Put the jar and tube in the box. Put clay around the tube to make it look like a volcano. Leave the top open.

Take your volcano outside, or put it in a sink or tub. Pour the red vinegar down the hole. Stand back and watch your volcano erupt!

Things You Need:

- vinegar
- measuring cup
- narrow jar
- red food coloring
- baking soda
- cardboard box
- modeling clay
- cardboard
- tape

Volga River

The Volga (*VAHL guh* or *VOHL guh*) River is the longest river in Europe. It flows 2,300 miles (3,700 kilometers) through western Russia. The Volga begins in the Valdai Hills, about 200 miles (320 kilometers) southeast of St. Petersburg. It then flows southward to the Caspian Sea.

Most of the Volga is frozen for three months of each year. Canals connect the river with the Baltic Sea, the White Sea, and the Black Sea by way of the Sea of Azov.

Farmers grow wheat in the river valley. The area is also rich in minerals and is the center of a large oil industry.

The Volga River flows southward through Russia to the Caspian Sea.

Volleyball

Volleyball is one of the world's most popular sports.

Volleyball is a game in which the players hit a ball back and forth across a net with their hands or arms. It is one of the world's most popular sports. Volleyball is played in the Olympic Games.

There are two main kinds of volleyball. Indoor volleyball is played indoors on a court often made of wood. There are six players on each team. Outdoor volleyball is played outdoors on a sand or grass court. There may be two, three, four, or six players on each team. This article is about indoor volleyball.

The volleyball is round. A net hangs across the center of the court, which is shaped like a rectangle. The net is 7 feet $4\frac{1}{4}$ inches (2.2 meters) high for women's games and slightly higher for men's games.

The game starts with a serve by a person in the right back corner of the court. The server hits the ball with an arm or a hand. The serve must pass over the net into the other team's court. Players return the ball by hitting it with their hands or arms. The players on each team try to hit the ball to the floor of the other team's court. They also try to make it hard for the other team to hit the ball back.

In most games, only the serving team can score. It scores a point each time the ball touches the other team's floor. It also scores a point if the other team hits the ball more than three times or hits the ball out of bounds. A team loses the serve if the served ball hits the net or goes out of bounds. The first team to score 15 points wins, but it must win by at least two points.

William G. Morgan, a physical-education teacher at the YMCA in Holyoke, Massachusetts, invented volleyball in 1895. Today, the game is most popular in Asia, Europe, and South America.

Volleyball players bat a ball back and forth across a high net. They often leap high to spike a ball, or drive it downward.

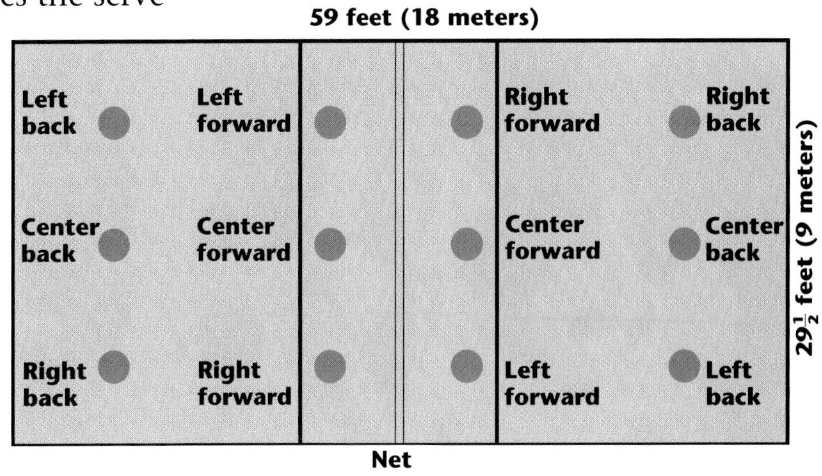

An indoor volleyball team has six players. Each player plays in a different position, *above*.

Volume

The volume (*VAHL yuhm*) of something is the amount of space it takes up. Both solids and liquids have volume.

The volume of a solid, such as a book, is found by multiplying the length of the book by its width and height. Solids may be measured in cubic feet or cubic meters.

The volume of a liquid, such as water, is often measured in special containers that have marks showing different volumes. Many people in the United States measure liquid volume in gallons, quarts, pints, and fluid ounces. A gallon equals 4 quarts, a quart equals 2 pints, and 1 pint equals 16 fluid ounces. In the metric system, liquids are measured in milliliters and liters. One liter equals 1,000 milliliters.

Volume is the amount of space taken up by something. Volume can be measured in different ways.

Voting

Voting is a method by which groups of people make decisions. For example, people may vote to choose the leaders of their government. They may vote on whether to build a new school, hire more police officers, or raise tax money for a special project. Voting is one of the most important rights in the United States, Canada, and many other countries.

Some nations have elections, but they do not give people any real choice in voting. In a number of these countries, people may vote, but only for people named by the country's leadership.

Women in Wyoming voted in the 1888 election for president. But women in other parts of the United States were not allowed to vote until 1920.

Who may vote

Today, citizens age 18 or older may vote in Canada and the United States. In the United States, a person must also be registered to vote. When a person registers, his or her name is put on a list of people allowed to vote. On election day in most states, election judges check each person's name against the list before they let the person vote.

At one time, some U.S. citizens were not allowed to vote. African Americans were not allowed to vote until 1870, five years after the end of the American Civil War (1861-1865). Even then, some whites found ways to keep many African Americans from voting. Women were not allowed to vote in most states until 1920. Today, the United States and some other countries have laws to protect the voting rights of the people.

Many governments take away a person's right to vote in special cases. In the United States, people in prison for committing certain crimes are not allowed to vote.

Methods of voting

The United States and Canada use the Australian ballot system. Under this system, each voter marks a printed ballot while alone in a special voting booth. Many voters in the United States use voting machines. A voting machine records and counts votes during an election. It gives the voter a secret ballot and then immediately records how the person voted.

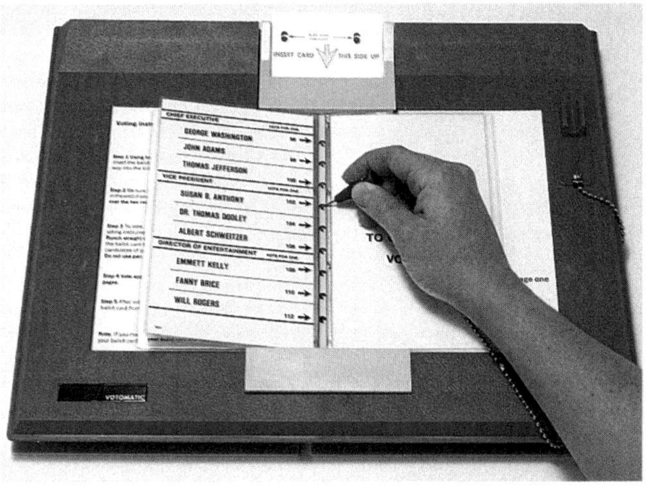

Some votes are counted by computer. To vote, the voter punches holes in a ballot. Later, a computer adds up the votes on the ballots and prints the totals.

Vulture

A vulture (*VUHL chuhr*) is a large bird that eats dead animals. Vultures' feathers are brown, black, or white. Most vultures have no feathers on their head and neck. They have good eyesight and can fly very well. All vultures have a hooked beak.

The king vulture is one of the most unusual vultures. It has orange, wrinkled skin on its head.

The largest vulture is the Andean condor. It has a wingspread of about 10 feet (3 meters). Its body measures up to 55 inches (139 centimeters) long.

Vultures live on every continent except Australia and Antarctica. They often live in groups. They build nests on the ground under cliffs, in logs, and in caves. Both parents care for the young.

Turkey vulture

Black vulture

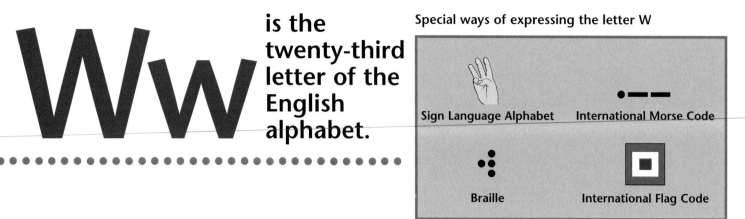

Ww is the twenty-third letter of the English alphabet.

Special ways of expressing the letter W

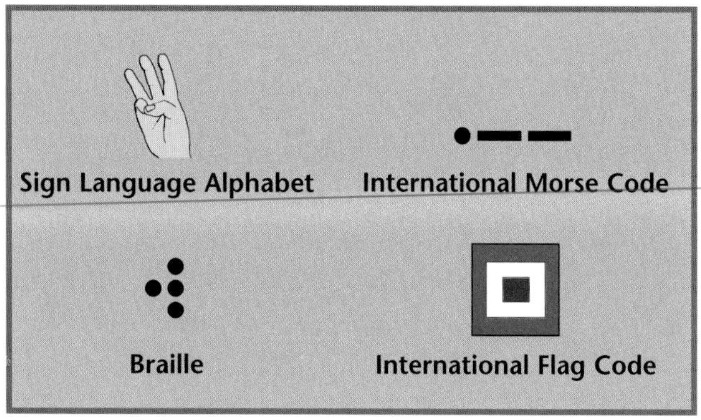

Development of the letter W

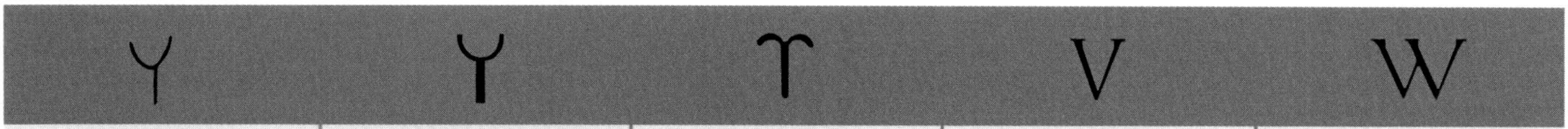

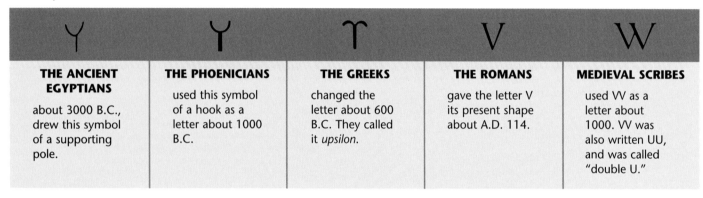

THE ANCIENT EGYPTIANS	THE PHOENICIANS	THE GREEKS	THE ROMANS	MEDIEVAL SCRIBES
about 3000 B.C., drew this symbol of a supporting pole.	used this symbol of a hook as a letter about 1000 B.C.	changed the letter about 600 B.C. They called it *upsilon*.	gave the letter V its present shape about A.D. 114.	used VV as a letter about 1000. VV was also written UU, and was called "double U."

Wagner, Richard

Richard Wagner

Richard Wagner (*VAHG nuhr*) (1813-1883) was the most important German opera composer of the 1800's. A composer writes music. Wagner wrote the words for his operas as well as the music. Wagner's operas include *The Flying Dutchman* (1843), *Lohengrin* (1848), *Tristan and Isolde* (1865), and *The Ring of the Nibelung* (1876).

Wagner was born in Leipzig, in what is now Germany, on May 22, 1813. His first complete opera was *The Fairies* (1834). Wagner made all the parts of an opera equally important. For example, the singing was just as important as the music. He also used melodies to go along with certain characters, places, or ideas each time they appeared.

Other articles to read: **Opera.**

Wales

Wales (*waylz*) is part of the United Kingdom of Great Britain and Northern Ireland. It is one of the four parts of the United Kingdom. The other three parts are England, Northern Ireland, and Scotland. Cardiff is the capital and largest city of Wales.

Wales lies on the west coast of Great Britain. It is bordered on the north by the Irish Sea, on the south by the Bristol Channel, and on the west by St. George's Channel and Cardigan Bay. England lies to the east.

Land. Wales is a land of great beauty. The Cambrian Mountains cover about two-thirds of the land. In central and southern Wales are large, flat plateaus (*plah TOHZ*) cut by deep valleys. On the plateaus are forests, pastures, grassy plains, moors (open wasteland), and bogs (swamplands). Small lakes and waterfalls abound.

People. Although Wales has been joined with England for more than 400 years, the Welsh have kept their own language, literature, and traditions. Welsh is one of the oldest languages in Europe. Welsh literature and music also are among the oldest in Europe.

In general, the way of life in Wales is much the same as in the rest of Europe and in the United States. For example, many people like to relax by watching television. But

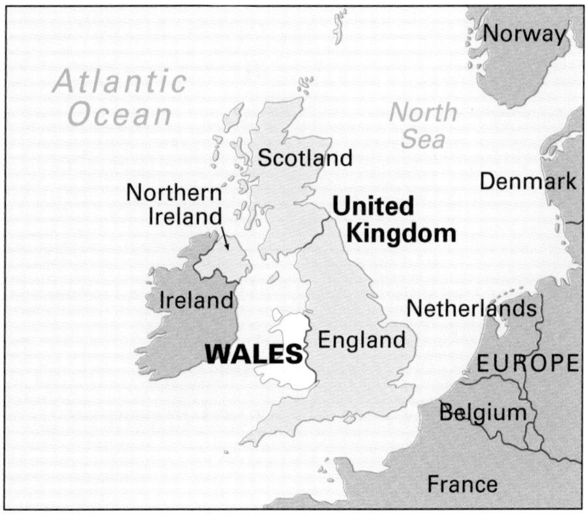

Wales and its neighbors

Facts About Wales

Capital: Cardiff.

Area: 8,015 sq. mi. (20,758 km^2).

Population: Estimated 2006 population—2,992,000.

Official languages: Welsh and English.

Climate: Mild, with warm summers and some cold weather in winter. Sea winds bring plenty of rain the year around.

Chief products:

Agriculture: barley, cabbage, cattle, cauliflower, hay, oats, potatoes, sheep.

Manufacturing: aluminum, chemicals, electrical and electronic equipment, iron and steel, motor vehicle and airplane parts, petroleum products, plastics, steel, synthetic fibers, tin plate.

Mining: coal, limestone, slate.

Form of government: Political division of the United Kingdom.

Welsh people have also kept older customs alive. For example, on the feast of Saint David, who is believed to protect Wales, the people wear the traditional symbols of Wales—the leek and the daffodil.

Llynnau Mymbyr, Snowdonia, Wales

Most Welsh people live in towns, cities, and factory areas in southern Wales. Most are Protestant Christians.

Rugby football is the most popular sport in Wales. Almost every town and village has its own team. Other popular sports are soccer and cricket.

Welsh cooking is simple. A favorite dish is Welsh rarebit, made of melted cheese on toast.

Resources and products. In the past, coal mines and metal factories provided many jobs. Today, many Welsh people have service jobs. They work in banks, schools, hospitals, and other businesses.

History. More than 200,000 years ago, prehistoric people lived in caves in northeastern Wales. Over time, many different peoples controlled the area, including the Celts and the Romans. The English gained control in the 1200's. King Henry VIII of England joined Wales and England under a single government in 1536. In 1999, the government of the United Kingdom allowed Wales to establish a National Assembly to handle local Welsh matters.

Walker, Alice

Alice Walker (1944-) is an African American author who writes about black and white people who live in America and Africa. In her stories, Walker creates happy communities of blacks in which women are powerful figures. Walker has been praised for having strong black women in her stories.

Walker has written a number of books. *The Color Purple* (1982) won an award called the Pulitzer Prize in 1983. She also has collections of poems. Other writings include speeches and letters about problems between blacks and whites. Walker's writings also talk about her experiences as a black woman in America.

Walker was born in Eatonton, Georgia. She was the youngest of eight children.

Alice Walker

Wallabies

Wallaby

A wallaby (*WAHL uh bee*) is an animal that looks like a small kangaroo. A wallaby has large feet, long back legs, and small front legs. It hops like a kangaroo. Wallabies vary in size. One of the largest wallabies grows more than 5 feet (1.5 meters) long and weighs up to 60 pounds (27 kilograms).

Wallabies live in the grasslands and forested areas of New Zealand and Australia. They eat mainly grasses.

A wallaby is a marsupial (*mahr SOO pee uhl*). Marsupials are animals that give birth to tiny babies. As soon as they are born, the babies crawl into a pouch on the mother's belly. There, they drink the mother's milk until they are bigger and stronger.

Walrus

Walruses

A walrus is a sea animal that lives in oceans in the Far North. A large walrus grows about 12 feet (3.7 meters) long and weighs up to 3,000 pounds (1,400 kilograms). It has short, stiff hairs on its upper lip, two long ivory tusks, and flat flippers on its four feet. The tusks are long upper teeth. The walrus uses its tusks as hooks when it climbs onto ice. It also uses them to fight polar bears. The walrus uses its flippers to swim.

During the winter and spring, walruses drift on large floating blocks of ice. In summer, some may rest on shore. A walrus spends much time in the water searching for clams, its favorite food.

War of 1812

The people of Washington, D.C., fled the city as British troops burned the Capitol and other buildings on August 24, 1814.

The War of 1812 (1812-1815) was fought between the United States and Great Britain. The U.S. government gave two main reasons for declaring war. It said that the British Royal Navy was causing problems with U.S. trading ships going to France. The United States said British ships stopped American ships and took away sailors of British birth. Some people also believed that Britain was encouraging American Indians to attack American pioneers moving westward.

Neither side did better than the other early in the war. Americans tried to take over Upper and Lower Canada, which are now Ontario and Quebec, but failed. On August 24, 1814, British troops attacked Washington, D.C. They burned the Capitol and other government buildings. Many American volunteers rushed into service and helped stop the attack.

The war ended in 1815. Neither side won.

Warhol, Andy

Andy Warhol (*WAWR hawl*) (1930?-1987) was an American artist. He was part of the art movement called Pop Art, which made art out of everyday objects. Warhol is best known for his simple, colorful pictures of famous people and such everyday objects as soup cans and soft-drink bottles. Sometimes, he made these pictures very large or used unusual colors for these objects and people. He often repeated images many times in a single picture.

Warhol was born in Pittsburgh, Pennsylvania. He graduated from the art school of the Carnegie Institute of Technology in 1949. Warhol then moved to New York City, where he became a successful commercial artist. Later, he became known as a painter. He also made films.

Andy Warhol stands in front of his double portrait of Hollywood star Marilyn Monroe. Warhol painted many portraits of famous people.

Wart hog

A wart hog is an African pig. It lives in dry, forested areas where it can hide in the shrubs. It is about 30 inches (76 centimeters) high at the shoulder and may weigh more than 200 pounds (90 kilograms). A wart hog has long, curved tusks and a huge, flat head. Between its tusks and its eyes are the three pairs of large "warts" that give the hog its name. It has light gray skin with stiff, brownish-gray hairs. Long, stiff hair hangs over its back and head.

The wart hog travels in small family groups. But old male wart hogs usually live by themselves. Wart hogs eat roots, plants, birds' eggs, and small animals.

Wart hog

Washington

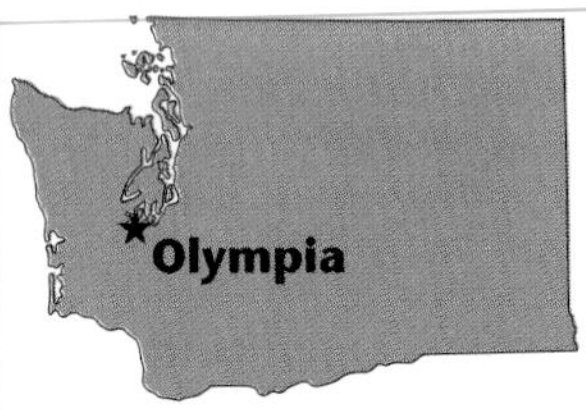

Washington (blue) ranks 20th in size among the states.

State flag

State seal

Washington is a state in the Pacific Coast region of the United States. It lies along the Pacific Ocean between Canada and Oregon. Idaho lies to the east. Washington is called the *Evergreen State*. Its thick forests of fir and pine trees stay green the year around.

Olympia is the capital of Washington. It is an important port on the south shore of Puget Sound. Puget Sound is a large waterway that flows into Washington from the Pacific Ocean. Seattle, Washington's largest city, lies on the south shore of Puget Sound. Seattle is a major business center for the Pacific Northwest region.

Seattle is a major business center of the Pacific Northwest region. Mount Rainier rises southeast of the city.

Land. The rugged Olympic Mountains are in the northwest. Mount Rainier is the highest peak in Washington. The Cascade Mountains stretch down the middle of the state. The Cascades include several volcanoes. One of them, Mount St. Helens, erupted in 1980. The area around Puget Sound is a lowland plain. Most of the people in Washington live there.

The Columbia River flows south through the state, then along the border into the Pacific Ocean. The Columbia Plateau covers most of central and southeastern Washington. It is made of hardened lava, or melted rock. This region has dry canyons with steep walls called coulees (*KOO leez*). There are also scablands, patches of hard lava on the ground.

Resources and products. Washington makes airplanes, space rockets, and ships. Food-processing plants pack fish and meat as well as frozen fruits and vegetables. Fishing fleets catch salmon, halibut, and many other kinds of fish off the coast.

Washington's forests provide timber for making paper and wood products. Farmers in eastern Washington grow wheat, oats, and barley. They also plant potatoes, asparagus, carrots, peas, and other vegetables. Washington grows more apples than any other state.

Important dates in Washington

Indian days	The Chinook, Nez Perce, and Yakima Indians lived in the Washington region before European people arrived.
1775	Bruno Heceta and Juan Francisco de la Bodega y Quadra of Spain became the first Europeans to land on Washington soil.
1792	Captain Robert Gray, an American, sailed into Grays Harbor and the Columbia River. English explorer George Vancouver traveled along the coast of Washington and Puget Sound.
1805	American explorers Meriwether Lewis and William Clark reached Washington and the Pacific Ocean.
1810	A British-Canadian fur-trading post was established near what is now Spokane.
1818	Britain and the United States agreed that citizens of both countries could trade and settle in the region.
1853	Congress created the Washington Territory.
1855-1858	Indian wars were fought in the Washington Territory.
1883	The Northern Pacific Railroad linked Washington and the East. This railroad brought many settlers to the area.
1889	Washington became the 42nd U.S. state on November 11.
1909	The Alaska-Yukon-Pacific Exposition was held in Seattle.
1942	Grand Coulee Dam was finished.
1974	Expo '74, a world's fair, was held in Spokane.
1980	Mount St. Helens volcano erupted, killing 57 people and causing much damage in southwestern Washington.
1996	Gary Locke of Washington became the first Chinese American to be elected governor of a U.S. state.

The Treaty of Oregon fixed the boundary between Washington and Canada at latitude 49° in 1846.

Other articles to read: **Lewis and Clark expedition; Mount Saint Helens.**

Facts About Washington

Capital: Olympia.

Area: 68,126 sq. mi. (176,446 km^2).

Population: 5,894,121.

Year of statehood: 1889.

State abbreviations: Wash. (traditional), WA (postal).

State motto: *Alki* (an Indian word meaning *Bye and Bye*).

State song: "Washington, My Home." Words and music by Helen Davis.

Largest cities: Seattle, Spokane, Tacoma.

Government:

State government:

Governor: 4-year term.
State senators: 49; 4-year terms.
State representatives: 98; 2-year terms.
Counties: 39.

Federal government:

U.S. senators: 2.
U.S. representatives: 9.
Electoral votes: 11.

State bird
Willow goldfinch

State flower
Coast rhododendron

Washington, Booker T.

Booker T. Washington

Booker T. Washington (1856-1915) was the most important African American leader and educator of his time. Washington established Tuskegee Institute, a school for African Americans in Tuskegee, Alabama. He was the principal and a teacher at Tuskegee for 33 years.

Booker Taliaferro Washington was born a slave in Hales Ford, Virginia, near Roanoke. After the United States government freed all slaves in 1865, his family moved to West Virginia. There, Washington worked in coal mines. From 1872 to 1875, he was a student at Hampton Institute in Hampton, Virginia. The school was established in 1868 to help educate former slaves. Washington became a teacher there in 1879.

In 1881, Washington founded Tuskegee Normal and Industrial Institute (now Tuskegee University). The school taught carpentry, farming, and other jobs. It also trained teachers. At the time, many African Americans were poor. Washington believed that African Americans should learn a job skill. Then, if they worked hard, they could buy property and their lives would improve.

Washington became a well-known political leader. He gave advice to presidents and members of Congress and helped them settle problems between white people and black people. Washington wrote a book about his life called *Up from Slavery* (1901).

The U.S. Capitol, in Washington, D.C., is the place where Congress makes the nation's laws.

Washington, D.C.

Washington, D.C., is the capital of the United States. It is also one of the country's most beautiful and historic cities. Washington lies on the Potomac River between Maryland and Virginia. It is the only American city or town that is not part of a state.

Washington covers the entire area of the District of Columbia, an area of land that is controlled by the federal government. The D.C. in the city's name stands for District of Columbia. Every year, millions of people from the United States and other countries visit Washington.

Washington serves as the headquarters of the country's national government. The president of the United States, the members of Congress, and thousands of other people with government jobs work in the Washington area.

Visitors to Washington can see such important government buildings as the United States Capitol, where Congress meets, and the White House, where the president lives and works. People can also visit the Washington Monument, Lincoln Memorial, and other famous structures that are dedicated to heroes in U.S. history. Visitors also tour the many museums in Washington, which together contain the world's largest collection of items from America's past.

President George Washington chose the city's location in 1791. The city took the place of Philadelphia as the nation's capital in 1800. City planners named the city in honor of George Washington.

The Vietnam Veterans Memorial, in Washington, D.C., has black granite walls carved with the names of all Americans who died in the Vietnam War or are thought to be missing.

The Lincoln Memorial in Washington, D.C., honors President Abraham Lincoln. It is visited by many tourists throughout the year.

Washington, George

George Washington (1732-1799) was the first president of the United States. He served from 1789 to 1797. He was known as a strong and patient leader.

No American has been honored more than Washington. The nation's capital—Washington, D.C.—was named for him. The state of Washington is the only state named after a president. Many other places also bear his name.

George Washington

George Washington's home, Mount Vernon, in Virginia

Washington was born on a farm in Westmoreland County, Virginia, on February 22, 1732. His father died when he was 11 years old.

In 1749, Washington became a surveyor, someone who maps the land. At the age of 20, he became a soldier. He became widely known as a good soldier. In 1759, he married Martha Dandridge Custis. Washington then went to work for the colonial government.

From 1775 to 1781, he was leader of the Continental Army that won American independence from Great Britain in the Revolutionary War in America (1775-1783). In 1787, Washington served as president of the Constitutional Convention, the group that wrote the United States Constitution. On April 30, 1789, he became the nation's first president. He was reelected in 1792. As president, Washington helped solve many of the new country's problems.

Other articles to read: **Constitution of the United States; Revolutionary War in America; Washington, D.C.; Washington's Birthday.**

Washington's Birthday

Washington's Birthday is an American holiday that honors the first president of the United States, George Washington. Washington was born on February 22, 1732. People in the United States celebrate the holiday on the third Monday in February.

People first celebrated Washington's Birthday in the late 1700's. Today, some states also honor Abraham Lincoln and other presidents on the third Monday in February. In places where other presidents also are honored on this day, the holiday is known as Presidents' Day.

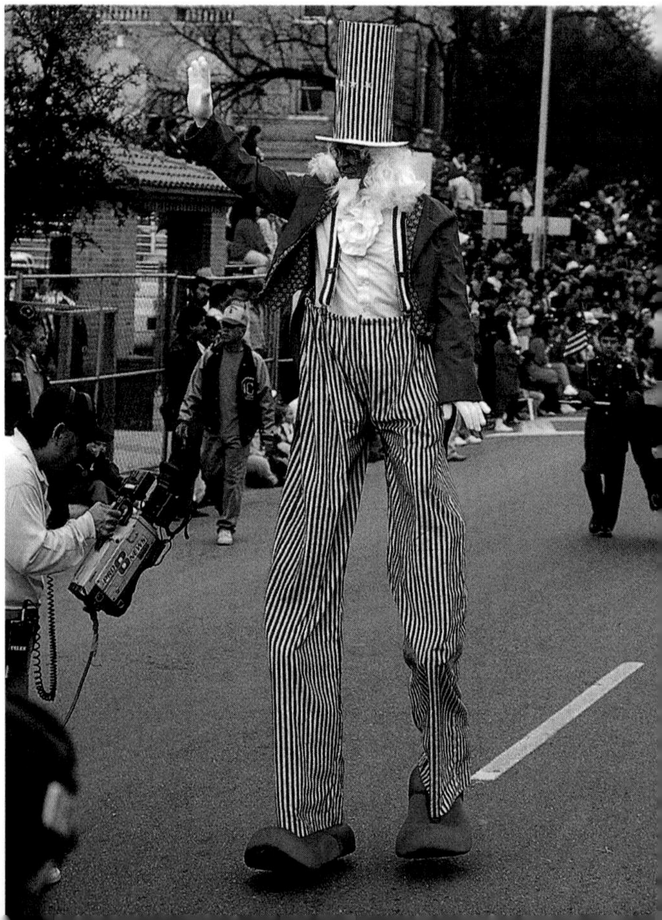

Washington's Birthday is sometimes celebrated with parades.

Wasp

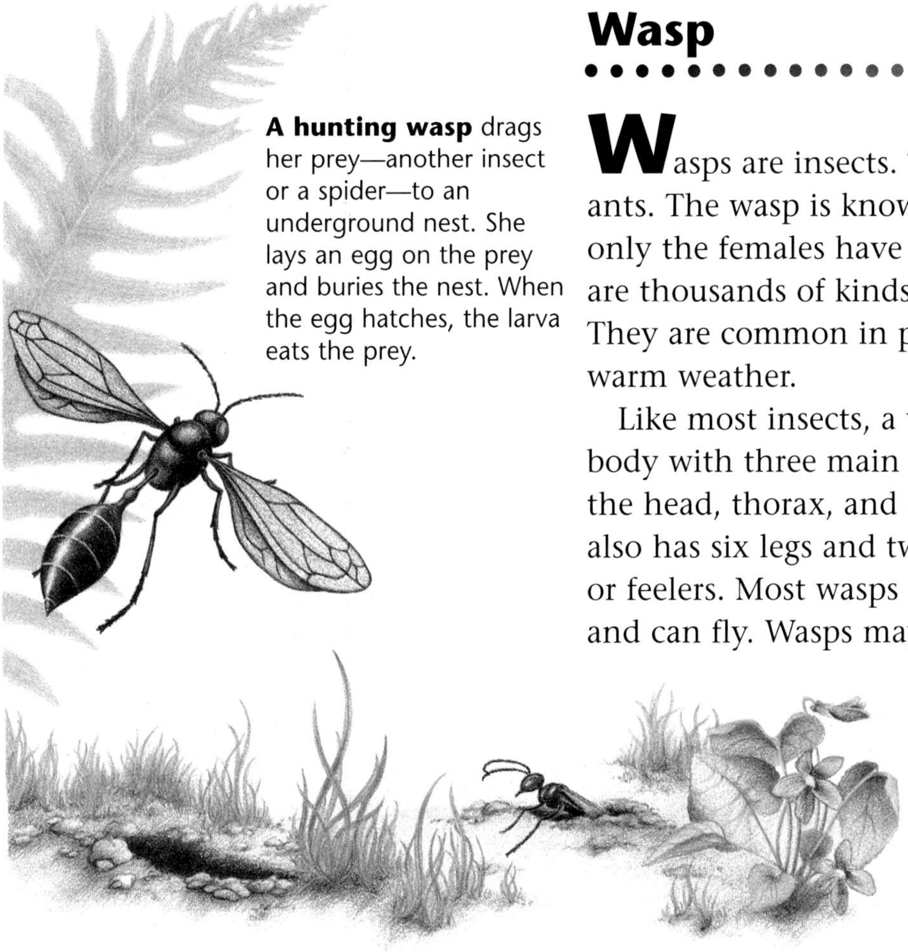

A hunting wasp drags her prey—another insect or a spider—to an underground nest. She lays an egg on the prey and buries the nest. When the egg hatches, the larva eats the prey.

Wasps are insects. They are related to bees and ants. The wasp is known as a stinging insect, but only the females have a sting. There are thousands of kinds of wasps. They are common in places with warm weather.

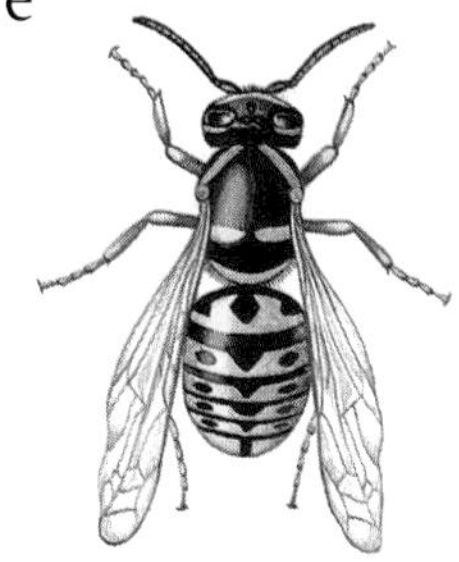

Queen yellow jacket

Like most insects, a wasp has a body with three main parts called the head, thorax, and abdomen. It also has six legs and two antennae, or feelers. Most wasps have wings and can fly. Wasps may be yellow or dark in color. Some have two colors, and others have stripes.

A wasp hatches from an egg as a larva, which looks like a tiny worm. When the larva reaches its full size, it spins a covering called a cocoon. Inside the cocoon, the larva changes into a pupa, and then into an adult wasp. The adult wasp drinks the nectar, or juice, of flowers. Some hunt insects and spiders to provide food for their young.

Wasps that live in family groups make their nests out of paper.

There are two main kinds of wasps. One kind lives mostly alone. This group includes digger wasps and mud daubers. These wasps dig nests in the ground or in hollow twigs, or build nests of mud.

The other kind of wasp lives in family groups. This kind includes hornets and yellow jackets. Each family group has a queen that lays eggs. Workers in the group build the nest and care for the young. They make their nests of paper. The females make the paper by chewing up plants or old wood.

Water

Water covers almost three-fourths of the earth's surface. Water is everywhere. It fills the oceans, rivers, and lakes. It is also in the ground and in the air we breathe. Most scientists believe that life began in the salty water of the sea.

Every living thing needs water to live. In fact, every living thing is made up mostly of water. Human beings can live without food for more than two months, but they can live without water for only about a week. Human beings must take in about $2\frac{1}{2}$ quarts (2.4 liters) of water a day. We get this water from things we drink or eat.

Water has been shaping the earth since the world began. Rain washes soil into rivers. The oceans pound against the shores and shape the cliffs. Rivers cut canyons through rock. Rivers also build up land where they empty into the sea. Huge sheets of frozen water called glaciers (*GLAY shuhrz*) carve valleys and wear down mountains.

Water also helps keep the earth from getting too hot or too cold. Land takes in and gives off heat from the sun quickly. But the oceans take in and give off the sun's heat slowly. So breezes from the oceans warm the land in winter and cool it in summer.

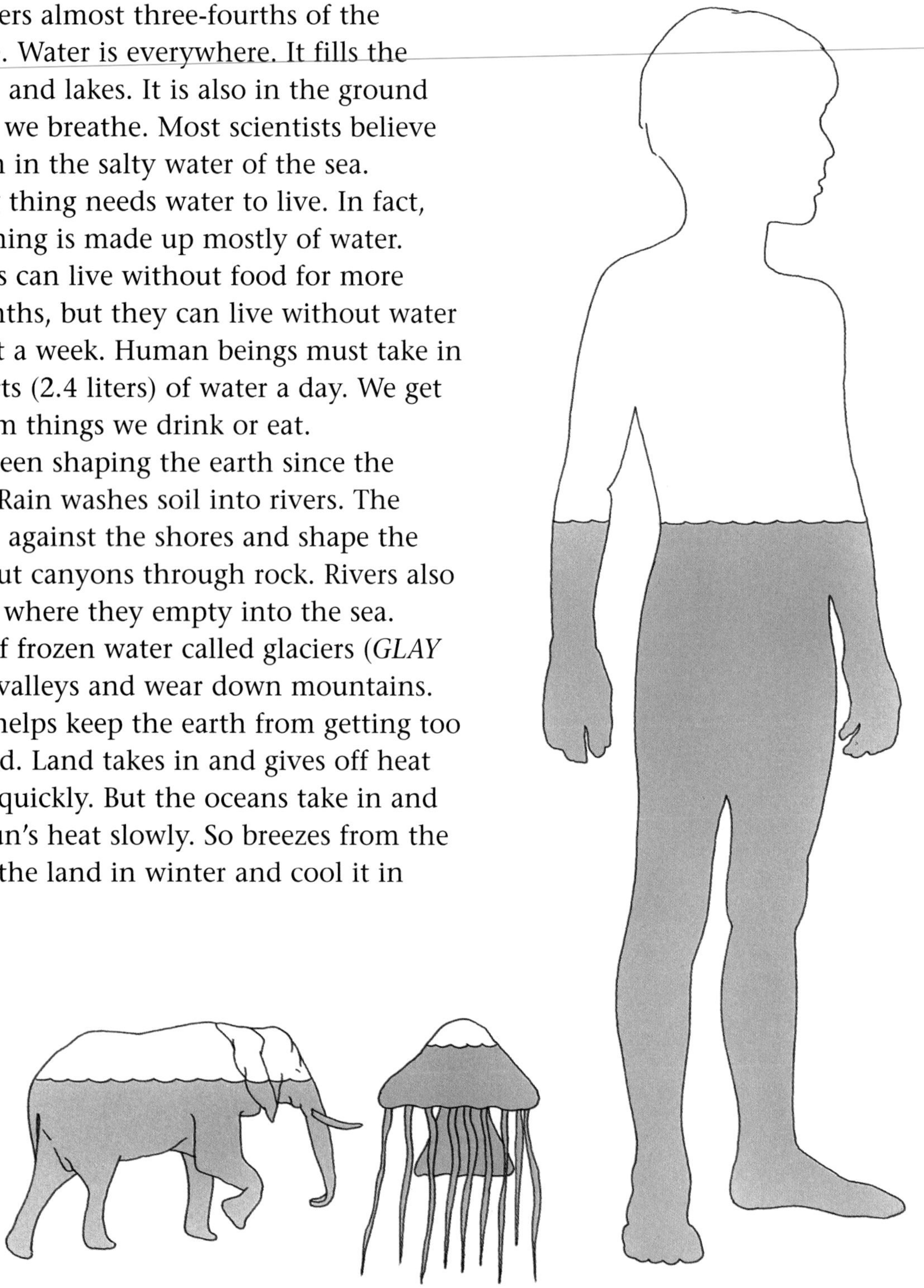

Living things are made up mostly of water. People are about two-thirds water. An elephant is almost three-quarters water. And a jellyfish is nearly all water.

Water on Earth is never used up. It is used and reused over and over again. Almost every drop of water we use finds its way to the oceans. There, it is turned into a gas called vapor by the heat of the sun. It then forms clouds and later falls back to the earth as rain. The rainwater drains into the oceans, and the series of changes starts over again.

Water in our daily lives

Throughout history, water has been important to people. We use water in our homes for cleaning, cooking, bathing, and carrying away wastes. We use water to grow food. Our factories use more water than any other material. We use the water in rushing rivers and waterfalls to produce electric power.

For people in many countries, however, getting enough water is not so easy. Millions of homes in Asia, Africa, and South America have no pipes carrying water into their homes. The people must haul buckets of water by hand from the village well or carry it in jars from pools and rivers far from their homes.

The water supply

Most of the world's water is in the oceans. Ocean water is too salty for drinking and farming. Only a little of the world's water is fresh water, which is not salty. Most of the world's fresh water is frozen in ice on mountains or in cold parts of the world.

Much of the world has plenty of fresh water, but some areas have too little.

Fresh water fills Medina Lake, Texas. But fresh water makes up little of Earth's total water supply.

Rain does not fall evenly over the whole earth. Some regions are always too dry, and others are too wet. Also, an area that usually gets enough rain may suddenly have no rain for a long time. Another area may be flooded with too much rain.

Some areas do not have enough water because the people waste it. Other areas have plenty of water, but some have no way to store it. Other areas have no way to make water clean for drinking. As our need for water keeps growing, we will have to make wiser use of our water supply. The more we learn about water, the better we will be able to do that.

Other articles to read: **Aqueduct; Canal; Cloud; Conservation; Dam; Dew; Environmental pollution; Evaporation; Flood; Fog; Frost; Geyser; Glacier; Hail; Humidity; Ice; Iceberg; Irrigation; Lake; Nutrition; Ocean; Plumbing; Rain; Snow; Water cycle; Waterfall; Wetland.**

Water buffalo

A water buffalo is a wild ox. This animal got its name because it likes to soak in pools of water for hours at a time. Many water buffaloes in Africa and Asia have been trained to plow fields and carry heavy loads. Wild water buffaloes can be dangerous.

Water buffaloes

Several kinds of water buffalo live in different parts of the world. The water buffalo of India may grow as big as $6\frac{1}{2}$ feet (2 meters) tall. The carabao (*kahr uh BAH oh*) of the Philippines is smaller. Both of these water buffaloes have long, rounded horns that grow out and back. They have thin hair and bluish-black skin.

Water cycle

The water cycle (*SY kuhl*) is the never-ending movement of the earth's water. Water goes from the oceans to the air to the land and back to the oceans again. For that reason, its movement is called a cycle.

This cycle begins when heat from the sun turns ocean water into water vapor. Water vapor is water that has become a gas. The water vapor rises high into the sky, where it cools off. The cooled water vapor changes into tiny drops of water. The drops are held up in the sky by rising warm air. When billions of these drops of water cluster together, they form a cloud. The water in the clouds eventually falls to earth as rain. If the water vapor is cold enough, it turns into ice and falls as snow. Most rain and snow falls into the ocean, but some falls on land. In time, this water also flows back to the ocean, and the cycle starts again.

Water is always traveling between the land, the air, and bodies of water. When you drink a glass of water, that water has passed through every part of the world—and will do so again and again.

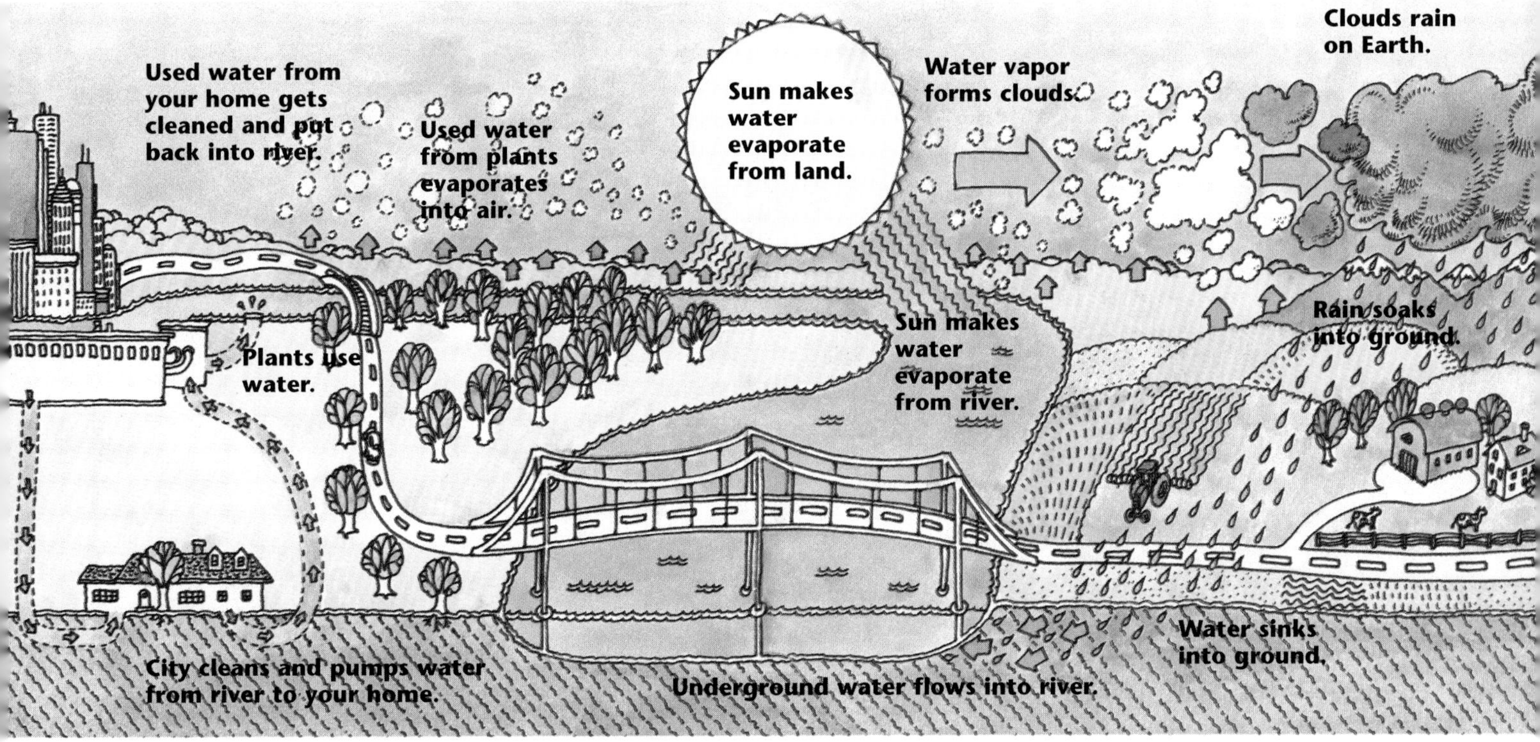
Used water from your home gets cleaned and put back into river.
Used water from plants evaporates into air.
Sun makes water evaporate from land.
Water vapor forms clouds.
Clouds rain on Earth.
Plants use water.
Sun makes water evaporate from river.
Rain soaks into ground.
Water sinks into ground.
City cleans and pumps water from river to your home.
Underground water flows into river.

The water you drink and bathe with today has been used and reused countless times over billions of years.

Because of nature's water cycle, there is as much water on Earth today as there ever was—or ever will be. Water changes only from one form to another, and moves from one place to another. The water you bathed in last night might have flowed in Russia's Volga River last year. Or perhaps Alexander the Great drank that water more than 2,000 years ago.

The water cycle is an important and wonderful process. It even helps cool the earth. As water evaporates, it takes in heat from its surroundings. After it takes in heat, it rises from the ground and takes the heat with it. Then the air feels cooler.

The water cycle also affects the weather. It creates the clouds that bring the rain and snow. Water from the rain and snow is necessary to all life on earth.

Other articles to read: **Cloud; Evaporation; Ocean; Rain; Snow; Water; Weather.**

Water pollution.

See **Environmental pollution.**

Water vapor

Water vapor is water in the form of a gas. It is always present in the air. Water vapor forms when heat from the sun causes water to enter the air from lakes, oceans, and rivers, or from moist soil and plants. As that happens, the water changes from a liquid to a gas. This change is called evaporation.

Air can hold only a certain amount of water vapor. But warm air can hold more water vapor than cool air can. When the air gets colder, some of the water vapor begins to change into tiny water droplets. These water droplets create fog near the ground or clouds high in the air.

Water vapor in the form of fog forms around Cades Cove in the Smoky Mountains in Tennessee.

Waterfall

Waterfalls are found where water suddenly falls from a high place to a low one. Many waterfalls are found in mountains. Sometimes a single waterfall forms, and sometimes a chain of them forms. Angel Falls in eastern Venezuela is the highest waterfall in the world. It has a total height of 3,212 feet (979 meters).

Waterfalls often form in places where rock is soft in one place and hard in another. A river wears down soft rock more quickly than hard rock, so that the soft rock becomes lower than the hard rock. If the hard rock is farther upstream than the soft rock, a waterfall may form.

Other articles to read: **Niagara Falls.**

Angel Falls in eastern Venezuela is the highest waterfall in the world. It has a total height of 3,212 feet (979 meters).

Watermelons

Watermelon

A watermelon is a large, sweet fruit. It has a smooth, hard outer skin called a rind (*rynd*), and it is juicy and sweet inside. Most watermelons have many seeds. The rind is striped or plain and ranges in color from gray-green to dark green. The inside may be white, greenish-white, yellow, orange, pink, or red. Some watermelons are round, while others are long. They are eaten in salads, as a snack, or as a dessert.

Watermelons grow on vines. A full-grown watermelon usually weighs 5 to 40 pounds (2.3 to 18.1 kilograms), but some weigh as much as 100 pounds (45.4 kilograms). A ripe watermelon makes a hollow sound when thumped.

Waves

Waves are movements that carry energy from place to place. Waves move through water, air, and other materials. They also move through areas where a force such as an electric force works. Waves are the up-and-down movements of water in the ocean. Sound and light also travel in waves. Television programs come to your house in waves.

People ride surfboards on the smooth part of an ocean wave, just below the crest.

It is easy to start a wave. If you throw a stone into a large, still pond, some movements will travel outward from the point where the stone entered the water. These will be a number of ring-shaped waves, each growing wider but all with the same center—the point where the stone hit the water. Energy produces the waves, and the waves carry energy.

Another simple wave experiment involves two people and a rope. Each person holds one end of the rope. When one person moves an end of the rope up and down sharply, energy moves from that person's hand and travels through the rope. As the energy passes through the rope, the rope moves up and down but not forward.

There are two main kinds of waves. Some waves travel in the same direction as the material they are traveling through. Sound waves are this kind of wave. When they travel through the air, they move in the same direction as the air. The second kind of wave moves in a different direction than the material it travels through. A rope wave is this kind of wave because the rope moves up and down while the wave moves from one end of the rope to the other.

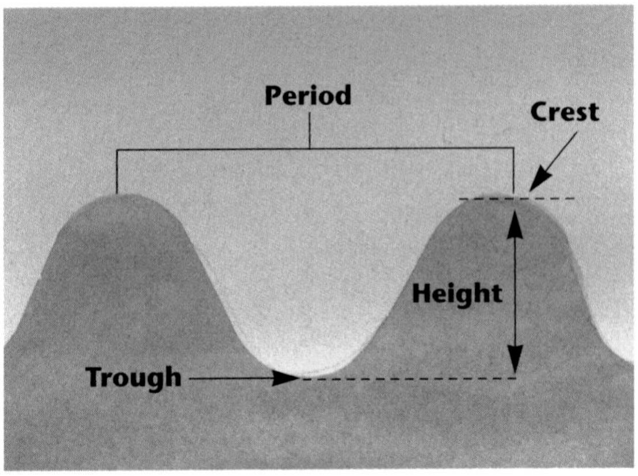

Waves are like hills and valleys. The top of each wave is the crest, and the low place between waves is the trough. The distance between the crests of the waves is the period, or wave length.

Weasel

A weasel is a small, furry animal with a long body, short legs, and small, round ears. The long-tailed weasel grows up to 18 inches (46 centimeters) long. Weasels live all over the world, except in Africa, Australia, and Antarctica.

Long-tailed weasel with summer coat

Most weasels have brown fur on the back and sides and light fur on the belly. In winter, the fur of weasels that live in cold places changes to white, except for a black-tipped tail. A white weasel hides easily in the snow.

Weasels usually hunt for food at night. They eat mice, squirrels, frogs, and other small animals. Like skunks, weasels spray a bad-smelling liquid when they are frightened.

Long-tailed weasel with winter coat

Weather

This weather map shows the weather predicted in different parts of the United States on a particular day. The map shows warm fronts as lines with half-circles attached; cold fronts as lines with triangles attached; areas of high and low pressure; the high and low temperatures predicted for many cities; and more.

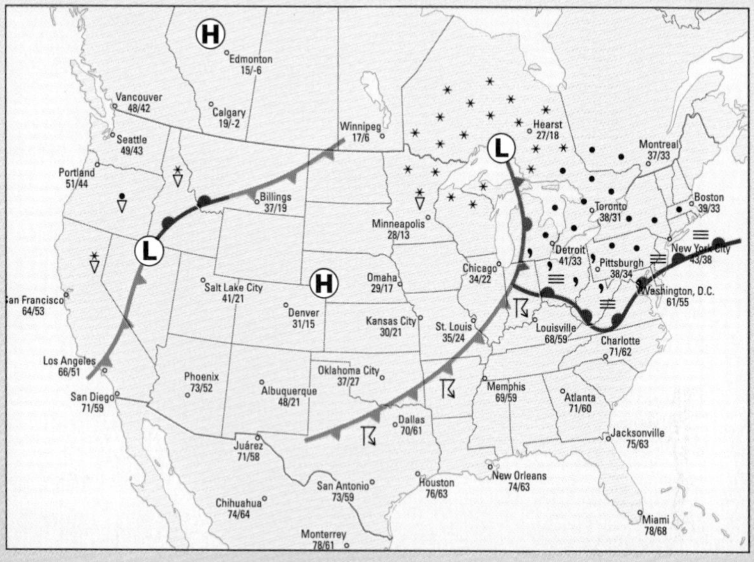

Weather is the condition of the air at a certain place and time. We describe the weather in many ways. For example, we may talk about the temperature of the air, whether the sky is clear or cloudy, how hard the wind is blowing, or whether it is raining or snowing. The weather may be warm and sunny in one place but cold and snowy somewhere else.

The earth has many kinds of weather conditions. The highest temperature ever measured and written down was 136 °F (58 °C) in Libya in 1922. The lowest temperature was −128.6 °F (−89.2 °C) in Antarctica in 1983. The driest place on earth is Arica, Chile. It hardly ever rains there. Arica once had no rain at all for 14 years.

The earth is not the only planet that has a variety of weather conditions. Every planet except Mercury has enough of an atmosphere (*AT muhs feer*) to have weather. An atmosphere is a layer of air around a planet. One of Saturn's moons, Titan, also has an atmosphere. However, this article is only about the weather on Earth.

Scientists who study the atmosphere and the weather are called meteorologists (*mee tee uhr AHL uh jihsts*). These scientists forecast the weather—they tell what the weather will be in the near future. Some meteorologists provide weather information for businesses. The best-known meteorologists are those who give weather reports on radio and TV.

Because Earth is tilted and spins around, large bodies of air and water in the northern half of Earth tend to move in a clockwise direction. That is, they move in much the same way as the hands of a clock. In the southern half of Earth, they tend to move in the opposite direction. This affects the movements of winds and ocean currents, which bring weather changes.

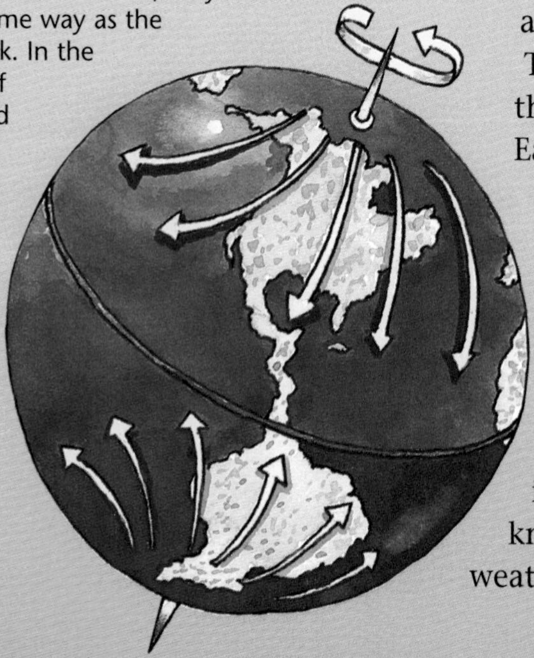

Weather terms

Air mass is a large body of air that has the same temperature and humidity throughout. Air masses can be wet or dry, cold or hot, cool or warm.

Air pressure is the weight of the air in our atmosphere pressing down on the earth.

Front is a narrow area where a cold air mass and a warm air mass meet. Most changes in weather happen along fronts.

High-pressure area is an area where the air pressure is heavy. High-pressure areas usually have clear skies.

Humidity is the amount of water vapor, or moisture, in the air.

Low-pressure area is an area where the air pressure is light. Low-pressure areas usually have cloudy skies.

Precipitation is any form of water that falls from clouds. Rain, snow, sleet, and hail are different kinds of precipitation.

Temperature is the measure of how hot or how cold the air is.

Wind is moving air.

The kind of weather a place usually has is called its climate (*KLY miht*). Scientists can tell what a region's climate is by looking at the plants that grow there as well as the temperatures and the precipitation (*prih SIHP ih TAY shun*). Rain and snow are two kinds of precipitation. Weather can change quickly, but changes in climate take many years.

When a warm front moves into an area, the warm air it brings rides up and over cold air. As the warm air rises, it cools and can hold less water. As a result, clouds may form or rain may fall.

What causes weather

Weather takes place in the atmosphere, the layer of air around the earth. Air is a mixture of gases and tiny bits of dirt and ash that are too small to be seen. The gases are about three-fourths nitrogen and one-fourth oxygen, with very small amounts of several other gases. These other gases include water vapor, an invisible gas that is produced when water evaporates. Water vapor forms clouds, rain, and snow.

Most weather takes place in the lowest part of the atmosphere, called the troposphere (*TROH puh sfeer*). It extends to about 10 miles (16 kilometers) above the ground. The three main things that

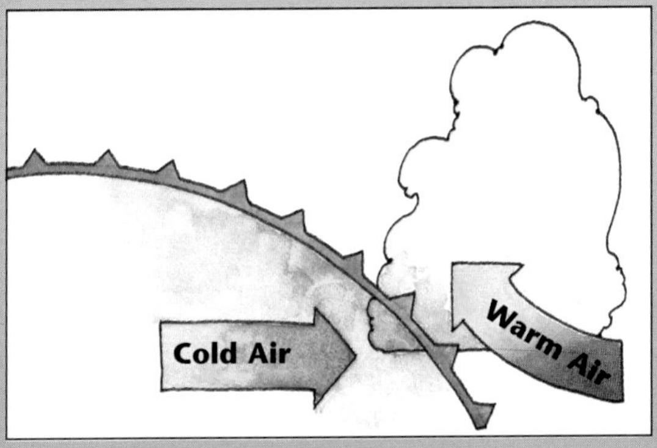

When a cold front moves into an area, it pushes warm air upward. As warm air cools, it can hold less water. Rain or snow often follows.

A Weather Calendar

Be a weather expert! Keep a calendar that shows the weather for every day.

Get permission to use the calendar. Turn it to the page for the month.

Cut some weather shapes from construction paper, such as round yellow suns, blue raindrops, gray clouds, and white snowflakes.

Every day, choose one or more shapes that show what the weather is like. Paste or tape the shapes on the square for the day.

Get the high and low temperature for the day from the newspaper, radio, or TV. Write them in the square. You can even write notes, such as, "Lots of snow fell. We couldn't get to school." Share your calendar with your family and friends.

Things You Need:

- calendar with a page for each month
- construction paper
- scissors
- pencil or marker
- tape or glue

Meteorologists use computers to track weather patterns and predict changes in the weather.

affect the weather in the troposphere are air temperature, air pressure, and humidity.

Air temperature depends partly on the sun. The rays of the sun warm the air. Thus, days are usually warmer than nights because the sun shines on the earth during the day.

Air pressure is the weight of the air. Air that is closer to the earth's surface is heavier than air that is farther up in the sky. Cold air is heavier than warm air, so it has higher pressure. Cold air sinks and warm air rises. This movement of the air is what we call the wind.

Humidity is water vapor in the air. Warm air can hold more water vapor than cool air can. However, air can hold only a certain amount of water vapor. When air has all the water vapor it can hold, the water vapor turns into droplets of water that form clouds. These droplets join together, and if they get big enough, they become raindrops and fall to the ground.

Meteorologists study large patterns of weather called weather systems. Some weather systems are brought by winds. Others include the movement of an air mass—a huge area of air that has about the same temperature and humidity.

The four main kinds of air masses are cold and dry, cold and humid, warm and dry, and warm and humid. When two air masses meet, a front forms. A warm front is the leading edge of a warm air mass, and a cold front is the leading edge of a cold air mass. A cold front often brings rain or snow with it.

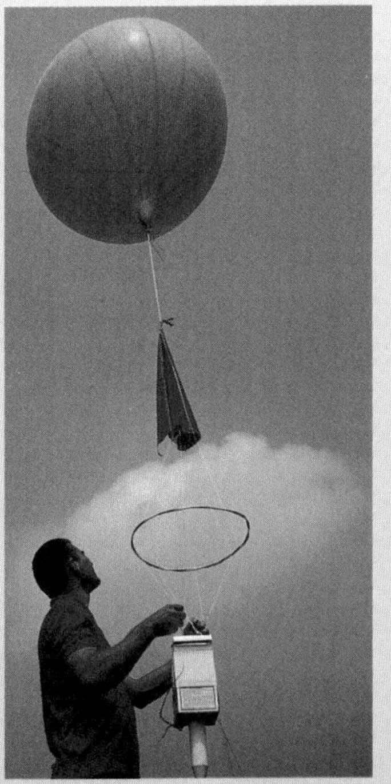

Weather balloons gather information about the atmosphere that can affect Earth's weather. This information, such as temperature or pressure, is sent to a radio station on the ground.

Measuring the weather

No single country can report on all the earth's weather all the time. Thus, the countries of the world must all work together to watch the weather. In 1873, a group of countries formed the International Meteorological Organization to share information about the weather. The organization changed its name in 1950 to the World Meteorological Organization.

Weather information comes from many different places. Observation stations check weather conditions from the ground. They use thermometers to measure air temperature and rain gauges to measure rainfall or snowfall. Weather balloons, airplanes, and ships provide information on the atmosphere above the earth's surface. Satellites in space provide weather information about large areas of the world.

Other articles to read: **Barometer; Climate; Cloud; Cyclone; Fog; Frost; Hail; Hurricane; Lightning; Monsoon; Rain; Season; Snow; Storm; Tornado; Wind.**

Some weather stations use radar to track how fast rain clouds and other air masses are moving, and where they are going. This can point to severe weather on the way.

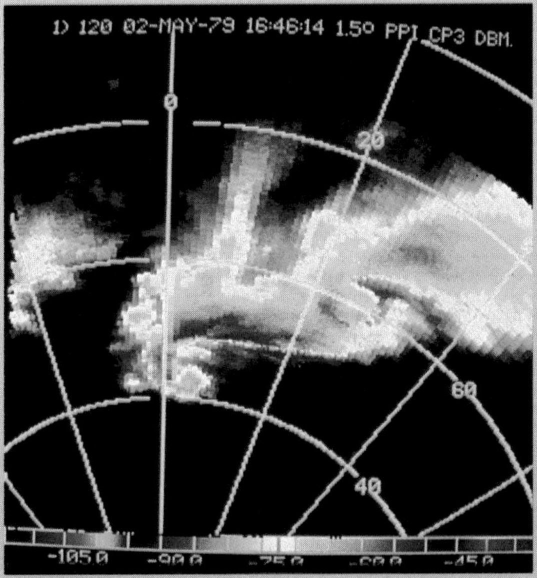

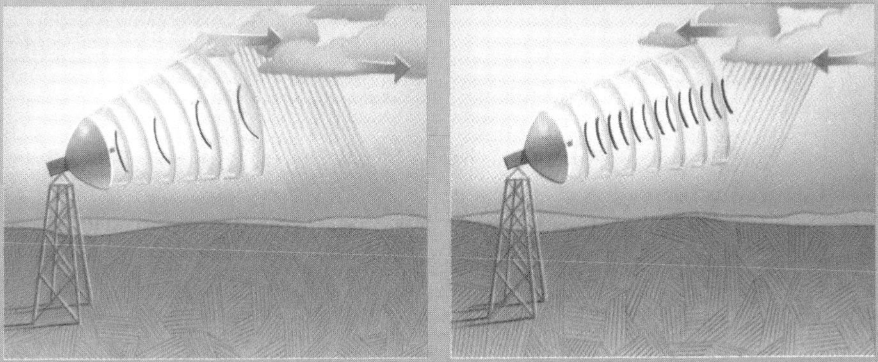

Weather radar tracks storms by sending out microwaves. The microwaves bounce off water drops or ice in the air. If the storm is moving away, *left,* the returning microwaves hit the radar gently. If the storm is coming closer, *right,* the microwaves hit the radar with more force.

Weaving

Weavers often use a machine called a loom to help them weave.

Weaving is a way of making cloth by crossing threads over and under one another. Many kinds of cloth and most blankets, clothing, and rugs are woven. Weavers use different types of thread, grasses, thin strips of wood or metal, and other materials.

All woven materials have two sets of threads. One set of threads runs up and down. These threads are called the warp. Another set of threads turns over and under the threads of the warp. These threads are called the weft. Weavers often use a machine called a loom to help them weave.

There are different types of weaves. In some, the weft goes over and under every warp thread. In others, the weft goes over and under two or more warp threads at a time. A weaver can also loop the weft yarns to make a rough cloth, such as terry cloth. Or a weaver may cut the loops to make a fuzzy cloth, such as corduroy. The weaver may create patterns in the cloth by changing the direction of the weave and adding colored threads.

Almost all looms weave cloth in much the same way. But there are many ways to weave without a

Different patterns are made by changing the colors of thread and by passing the weft thread over and under the warp thread in different ways.

In paper weaving, a person weaves strips of paper by hand.

loom, too. In paper weaving, a person weaves strips of colored paper by hand. In finger weaving, several pieces of cord tied together at one end make the warp. A longer cord is also attached to the warp. The weaver threads the long cord over and under the lengthwise pieces to make belts. Some artists weave reeds, yarn, and other materials through wire screens. The weaver can then bend the decorated screen into various shapes.

A simple loom can be made from a piece of cardboard. Evenly spaced notches are cut at the top and bottom of the cardboard to hold the warps in place. The weaver slips a stick under every other warp thread to make a space called a shed. A threaded needle easily passes through this space. The weaver then puts the stick under the other warp threads and repeats the process.

Other articles to read: **Tapestry.**

A simple loom can be used to weave yarn or strips of cloth.

Weed

A weed is any plant that grows where people do not want it to grow. A morning-glory in a farmer's crop is a weed, but a morning-glory in a garden is a lovely flower. Weeds cause problems in many ways. They keep other plants from getting enough sunlight and water, and they take food from the soil. They also carry insects and diseases that can hurt farm crops. Weeds can get in the way of cars, trains, and boats when they grow wild along roads, railroad tracks, and rivers. Some kinds of weeds are poisonous to human beings and other animals. Others can produce rashes on a person's skin or cause hay fever.

Dandelions in a yard are weeds.

There are many ways to get rid of weeds. People may cover the ground with grass clippings or

Queen Anne's lace is a weed. It is related to carrots, but its roots cannot be eaten.

wood chips to keep weeds from growing. Farmers may put insects and other small animals in the fields to eat certain weeds. Some people spray powerful chemicals on the plants to kill them. Others simply dig up the weeds.

Although weeds are pests in some places, they can be useful plants in other places. For example, such plants can help keep farm soil from blowing away when no crops are growing on the land. Animals may make their homes in weeds or eat the plants' seeds and leaves. People may also eat such plants or use them to make medicine.

Weightlifting

Weightlifting is the lifting of weights fastened to a rod called a barbell. People practice weightlifting for sport or exercise because it helps build strong muscles. Weightlifting is an event in the Summer Olympic Games.

In the sport of weightlifting, several people compete, or take part in a contest, to lift the most weight. They always compete against people of about the same size. There are two types of lifts—the snatch and the clean and jerk. In the snatch, the lifter quickly raises the bar above the head while squatting under it. In the clean and jerk, the lifter first brings the bar to the shoulders, then jerks the barbell over the head by quickly straightening the arms and legs.

Weightlifting is an event in the Summer Olympic Games. This weightlifter does the clean and jerk type of lift.

Weights and measures

Weights and measures are words we use to tell size, weight, temperature, and time. For example, people can measure the size of an object in inches or in centimeters. They can measure the weight of an object in pounds or in kilograms. A thermometer may show temperature in degrees Fahrenheit or in degrees Celsius. People tell time in seconds, minutes, and hours.

Measurements in inches and pounds belong to the inch-pound system. That system also includes feet, yards, and miles for measuring length or distance. It uses ounces for measuring small weights and tons for measuring large weights. People who use the inch-pound system measure temperature in degrees Fahrenheit.

Measurements in centimeters and kilograms

Units of measurement

To measure length or distance

1 foot	=	12 inches	=	about $30\frac{1}{2}$ centimeters
1 yard	=	3 feet	=	almost 1 meter
1 mile	=	5,280 feet	=	about $1\frac{3}{5}$ kilometers

To measure area

1 square foot	=	144 square inches	=	929 square centimeters
1 square yard	=	9 square feet	=	over $\frac{4}{5}$ square meter
1 acre	=	4,840 square yards	=	about $\frac{2}{5}$ hectare
1 square mile	=	640 acres	=	259 hectares

To measure volume

1 tablespoon	=	3 teaspoons	=	almost 15 milliliters
1 cup	=	16 tablespoons	=	237 milliliters or almost $\frac{1}{4}$ liter
1 pint	=	2 cups	=	473 milliliters or almost $\frac{1}{2}$ liter
1 quart	=	2 pints	=	946 milliliters or almost 1 liter
1 gallon	=	4 quarts	=	about $3\frac{3}{4}$ liters

To measure weight

1 pound	=	16 ounces	=	454 grams or almost $\frac{1}{2}$ kilogram
1 ton	=	2,000 pounds	=	907 kilograms or almost 1 metric ton

belong to the metric system. That system also includes meters and kilometers for measuring length or distance. It uses grams and milligrams for measuring small weights, and metric tons for measuring large weights. Temperature in the metric system is measured in degrees Celsius.

The United States is the only large country in which people still use the inch-pound system. The inch-pound system is sometimes called the customary system or the English system, though it is no longer used in England. People in England and nearly all other countries in the world now use the metric system.

Other articles to read: **Metric system.**

Welding

Welding is a way of using heat to stick pieces of metal together. Factories weld parts together to make cars, refrigerators, and other products. Builders weld huge pieces of metal to make parts for buildings and bridges. Other workers weld tiny pieces that make up parts for computers and other electronic products.

One way of welding is to fasten two pieces of metal together and heat them until they are partly melted. They stick together when the metal cools.

Heat for welding may come from burning gases blown out of a tool called a gas torch. Welding may also be done with electric current, which produces a very hot spark called an arc.

These welders are constructing a gas pipeline.

West Bank

The West Bank is a region between Israel and Jordan. Israel is a Jewish nation, and Jordan is an Arab nation, where most people are Muslims. Over the years, Arabs and Jews have fought for control of the West Bank.

The West Bank, Israel, and Jordan were all once part of Palestine, where the Jewish and Christian religions began. Palestine is also a holy place to the Muslims, who follow the religion of Islam. Muslims controlled the West Bank for hundreds of years.

Jordan took control of the West Bank in 1950, after a war between Arab nations and Israel. After a war in 1967, Israel took control. In the 1990's, Israel began to give control of the West Bank to the Palestinian Arabs who live there. But Israeli and Palestinian leaders could not reach a peace agreement. Violence broke out again in 2002. The Israeli government removed Jewish settlers from four West Bank settlements in 2005.

The West Bank and its neighbors

Other articles to read: **Gaza Strip.**

West Indies

The West Indies are islands that lie between the Caribbean Sea and the Atlantic Ocean. The islands stretch about 2,000 miles (3,200 kilometers) from near southern Florida in the United States to northern Venezuela in South America.

Three main island groups make up the West Indies. They are the Bahamas in the north, the Greater Antilles *(an TIHL eez)* near the center, and the Lesser Antilles in the southeast. The Bahamas have hundreds of small islands. The Greater Antilles include Cuba, the Dominican Republic, Haiti, Jamaica, and Puerto Rico. The Lesser Antilles are small islands southeast of Puerto Rico. People travel to the West Indies for the sunny weather and beautiful scenery.

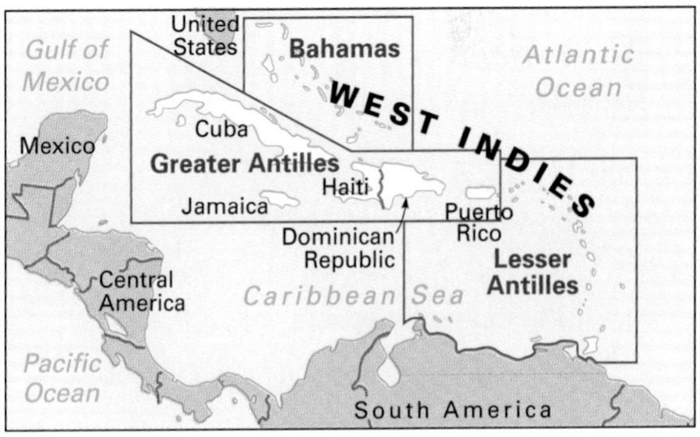

The West Indies and their neighbors

Other articles to read include those on the individual countries of the West Indies.

West Virginia (blue) ranks 41st in size among the states.

State flag

State seal

West Virginia

West Virginia is one of the southern states of the United States. It borders Ohio and Kentucky on the west, Virginia on the south and east, and Pennsylvania and Maryland on the north. West Virginia is called the *Mountain State* for its rugged mountain beauty.

Charleston is the capital and largest city. It lies in the southwestern part of the state. Charleston is the state's leading industrial center. Huntington, along the Ohio border, is the second largest city.

Lovely mountains, steep hills, and narrow valleys cover most of West Virginia.

Land. West Virginia is a mountainous state. Most of it is covered by thick forests. Beech, cherry, hickory, maple, oak, and poplar trees grow in West Virginia. Spruce, pine, and other trees stay green all the year around on the mountain slopes.

The Allegheny and Blue Ridge mountains stretch across the state's eastern border. This region has many caves and underground streams.

The Appalachian Plateau (*plah TOH*) covers the rest of the state. Swift-flowing streams cut narrow valleys around its rounded hills. The Ohio River flows along West Virginia's western border.

Resources and products. Minerals are West Virginia's most valuable natural resources. Coal is the state's most important mineral product. Natural gas fields lie under the western part of the state. Coal and natural gas are used for heating homes, running machines, and other purposes. West Virginia also mines limestone, oil, salt, and sand. Chemicals are the most important manufactured products.

Most farmers in West Virginia raise livestock, mainly chickens, beef cattle, and turkeys. Farmers also grow hay, corn, tobacco, and apples.

Important dates in West Virginia

Indian days	Indians living in the West Virginia region buried their dead in large mounds, many of which remain today.
1606	King James I of England gave the Virginia Colony to the Virginia Company of London, a business group. This colony included what is now West Virginia.
1660's	Many Indians in the area were killed by war and illness.
1727	Germans from Pennsylvania settled at New Mecklenburg (now Shepherdstown).
1742	John P. Salling and John Howard discovered coal on the Coal River.
1788	Virginia became a U.S. state. The new state included what is now West Virginia.
1836	The first railroad reached the West Virginia region.
1859	At Harpers Ferry, John Brown and his followers broke into the U.S. arsenal, a building where the government kept weapons. Brown wanted to help slaves fight their masters.
1861	During the Civil War, the counties of western Virginia refused to leave the United States with the rest of Virginia. Instead, these counties supported the Union, or the U.S. government.
1863	West Virginia became the 35th state on June 20.
Late 1800's	West Virginia became one of the leading U.S. mining states. By 1900, coal was the leading industry.
1968	Explosions and fire in a coal mine at Farmington killed 78 people. The disaster led to new mine safety laws.
1972	The Buffalo Creek flood, one of the worst in West Virginia history, caused more than 100 deaths.

Mound builders of various Indian groups built hundreds of burial mounds in the Ohio and Kanawha river valleys.

Other articles to read: **Mound builders.**

Facts About West Virginia

Capital: Charleston.

Area: 24,231 sq. mi. (62,759 km^2).

Population: 1,808,344.

Year of statehood: 1863.

State abbreviations: W. Va. (traditional); WV (postal).

State motto: *Montani Semper Liberi* (Mountaineers Are Always Free).

State song: "The West Virginia Hills."

Largest cities: Charleston, Huntington.

Government:

State government:
Governor: 4-year term.
State senators: 34; 4-year terms.
State delegates: 100; 2-year terms.
Counties: 55.

Federal government:
U.S. senators: 2.
U.S. representatives: 3.
Electoral votes: 5.

State bird
Cardinal

State flower
Rhododendron

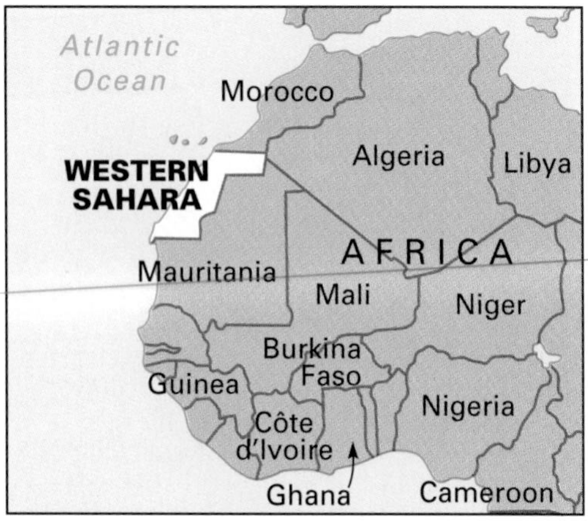

Western Sahara and its neighbors

Western Sahara is mostly covered by rocky desert.

Western Sahara

Western Sahara is an area on the northwest coast of Africa. It lies between Morocco, Algeria, Mauritania, and the Atlantic Ocean. Rocky desert covers most of the area.

Most of the people of Western Sahara are Arabs or people called Berbers. Most Arabs and Berbers are Muslims (*MUHZ luhmz*), people who follow the religion of Islam. Many of Western Sahara's people are nomads. They travel from place to place to find food for their camels, goats, and sheep. Some people fish along the coast.

Morocco and Spain have controlled the area at different times. Today, Morocco claims Western Sahara as part of Morocco. But many people who live in Western Sahara say they want to be independent.

Western Samoa. See **Samoa.**

Wetland

A wetland is a place where there is usually water near or above the surface of the ground. Wetlands are found throughout the world. Many kinds of plants and animals live in them.

The main kinds of wetlands include bogs, fens, marshes, and swamps. Bogs and fens are usually found in cold places. They have large amounts of springy, spongy soil called peat (*peet*). Bogs also have lots of acid in the soil. Many kinds of mosses grow in bogs and fens. Marshes and swamps are common in both warm and cold places. Marshes are found in the shallow waters of lakes and streams. Cattails, horsetails, and other plants grow in marshes. Swamps often develop in areas that are flooded only part of the year. Most swamps have trees and shrubs.

Wetlands are important in nature. They provide a home for many plants and animals, including alligators, beavers, birds, frogs, insects, muskrats, otters, salamanders, snakes, and turtles. Wetlands also help control flooding because they hold large amounts of water.

Many wetlands have been destroyed by people's activities. Almost half of the wetlands in the United States have been destroyed because people did not understand their value. Some swamps and marshes have been drained for farmland. Some wetlands have been polluted by industry. Today, most governments work to save the remaining wetlands in the world.

Other articles to read: **Marsh; Swamp.**

Wetlands are home to many animals, such as this nesting red-necked grebe.

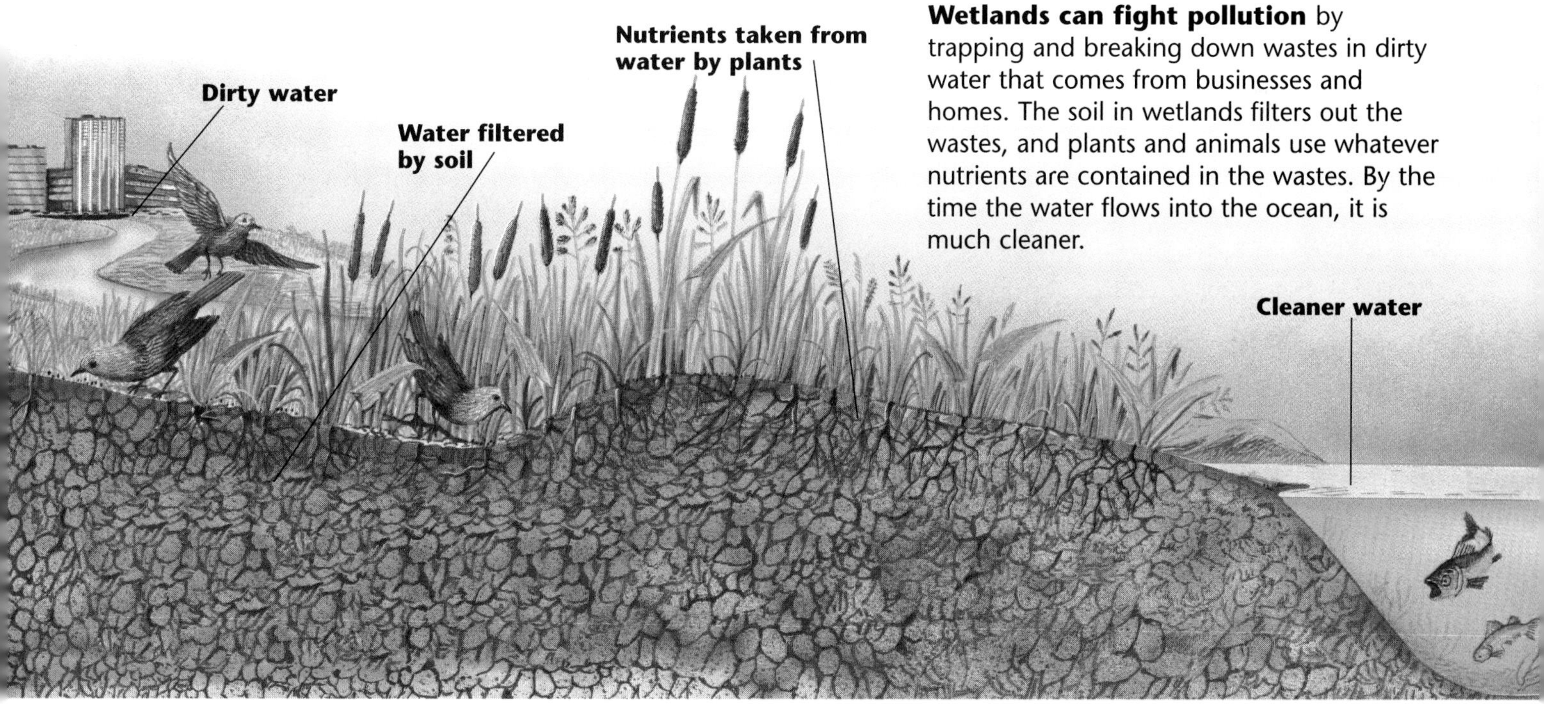

Wetlands can fight pollution by trapping and breaking down wastes in dirty water that comes from businesses and homes. The soil in wetlands filters out the wastes, and plants and animals use whatever nutrients are contained in the wastes. By the time the water flows into the ocean, it is much cleaner.

Whale

A whale is a huge sea animal that looks a lot like a fish. But it is not a fish. Instead, it is a kind of animal called a mammal. Mammals feed their young with mother's milk. Other mammals include chimpanzees, dogs, and human beings.

Most whales are enormous. One kind, the blue whale, is the largest animal that has ever lived. It grows up to 100 feet (30 meters) long and can weigh more than 150 tons (135 metric tons). Other kinds of whales are smaller. Some grow only 10 to 15 feet (3 to 5 meters) long.

The body of a whale

A whale has a long body, two side fins, and tail fins that spread from side to side. A whale swims by moving its tail fins up and down. It has smooth skin that may be black, brownish-gray, gray, or white. Some whales have patches of white on them. A whale has a few bristles, or short, stiff hairs, on its head. Beneath the skin, it has a layer of fat called blubber that helps keep it warm in the cold ocean waters.

Whales breathe through nostrils called blowholes at the top of the head. Some whales have one blowhole, and others have two. A whale comes to the surface to blow air out and breathe air in. When a whale lets out its breath, it shoots a big spray of air and water through the blowhole. A whale can hold its breath for a long time. Some whales can hold their breath underwater for up to two hours.

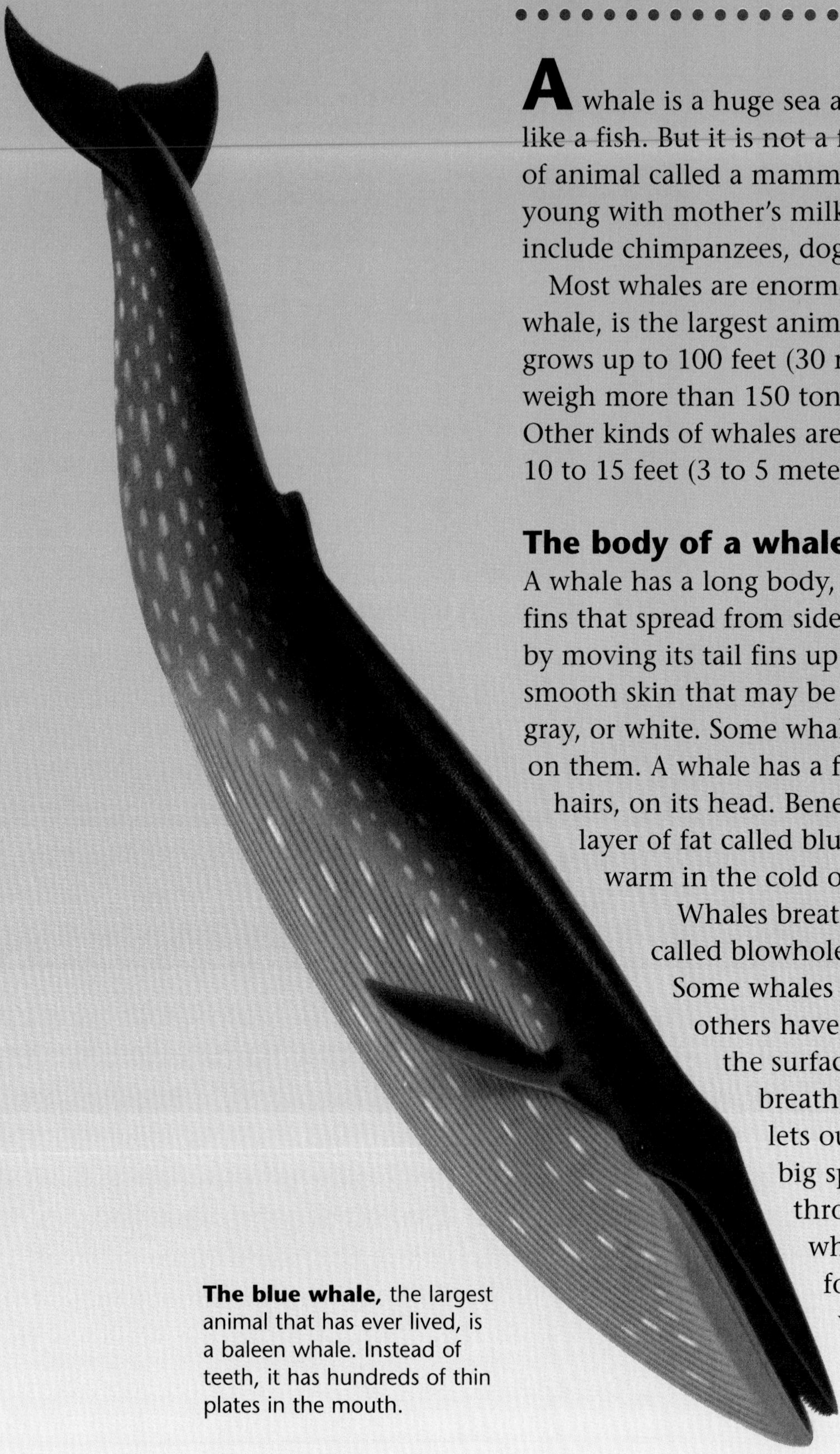

The blue whale, the largest animal that has ever lived, is a baleen whale. Instead of teeth, it has hundreds of thin plates in the mouth.

Kinds of whales

There are two main kinds of whales. They are baleen (*buh LEEN*) whales and toothed whales.

Baleen whales have no teeth. Instead, they have hundreds of thin plates called baleen in the mouth. The baleen is made of the same material as human fingernails. The baleen plates hang from the whale's upper jaw. Baleen whales eat by gulping mouthfuls of water containing small fish, tiny creatures called plankton, and other sea animals. They then force the water out through the baleen. The food gets trapped on the baleen, and the whale swallows it.

There are 10 kinds of baleen whales. They include bowhead whales and blue whales. Bowhead whales have a thick body, a huge head, and an arched mouth. Their baleen may grow as long as 13 feet (4 meters). Blue whales and some other baleen whales have a back fin. They can swim faster than other whales.

Toothed whales have teeth. There are about 65 kinds of toothed whales. They have different sizes and shapes. Most toothed whales eat fish or squid. Toothed whales include sperm whales, narwhals (*NAHR hwuhlz*), dolphins, and porpoises.

Sperm whales are the largest toothed whales. They grow up to about 60 feet (18 meters) long. A sperm whale has a huge, square head and a long, thin lower jaw. Only the lower jaw has teeth. These teeth fit into holes in the upper jaw.

Narwhals are unusual whales that live in the icy waters of the Arctic Ocean. The male has a tusk sticking out of its upper jaw. The tusk is about 8 feet (2.4 meters) long. It is the narwhal's only tooth. A few narwhals have two tusks. Most females have no tusks.

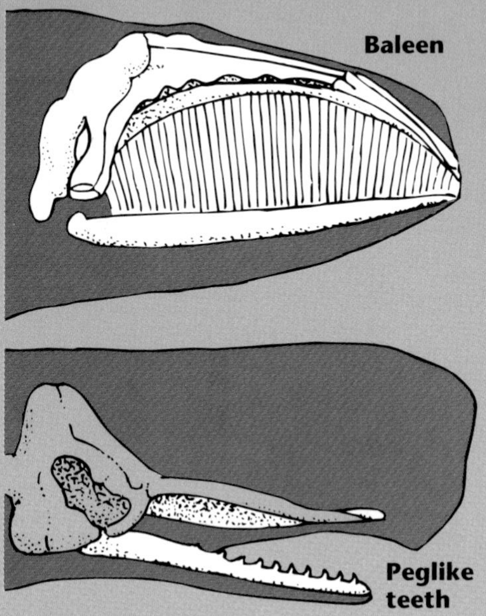

Baleen whales, *top,* have thin, bony plates that hang from the upper jaw. Toothed whales, *bottom,* have teeth like pegs.

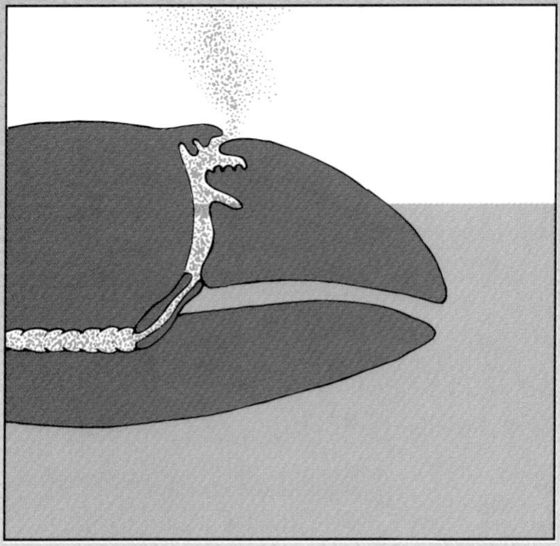

Whales have short, wide nasal passages that let them breathe quickly when they come to the surface. They breathe through blowholes on the top of the head.

A mother humpback whale swims with her baby, called a calf. Most whales have only one calf at a time.

Some kinds of whales leap from the water. The leaping action is called breaching.

Dolphins are smart animals with a snout like a beak. Porpoises look a lot like dolphins, but they have a rounded snout.

The life of a whale

Most whales have only one baby, called a calf, at a time. Even the calves are giant animals. A newborn blue whale weighs as much as a full-grown rhinoceros, and it is 23 feet (7 meters) long.

Mother whales protect their young. As soon as a calf is born, the mother gently pushes it to the surface to take its first breath. She stays close to it for at least a year and feeds it her milk. The rich whale milk helps the calf grow fast. Baby blue whales gain about 200 pounds (90 kilograms) per day.

Some toothed whales live in groups called herds, pods, or schools, but most baleen whales live alone or in small groups. Whales keep in touch with each other by making many kinds of sounds. They can hear these sounds over great distances.

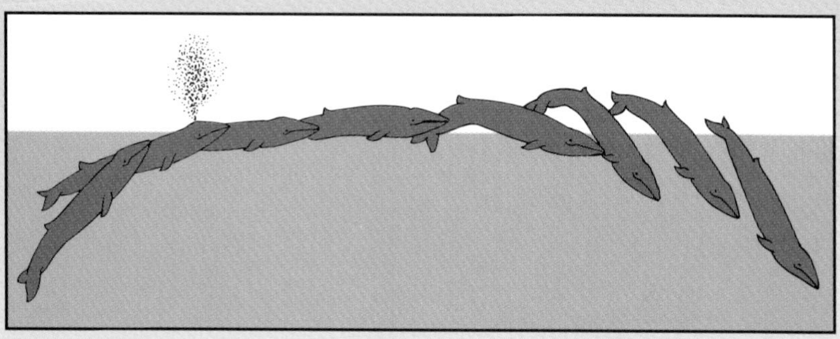

Whales can rise to the surface, breathe, and dive back into the water in one motion. This gives the whale only about two seconds to breathe in and out.

Some kinds of whales

Humpback whale

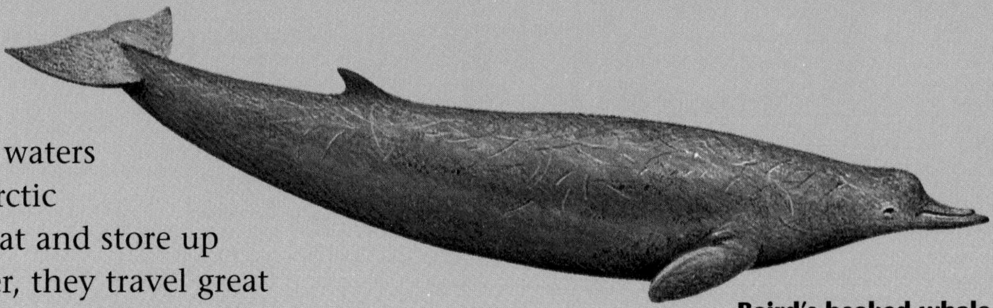

Baird's beaked whale

Most baleen whales spend summers in the cold waters of the Arctic or Antarctic oceans, where they eat and store up blubber. In the winter, they travel great distances to warmer seas. There, they mate and have babies. The next spring, they return home.

Sometimes whales swim onto shore. This action is called beaching. Beached whales cannot live long. Out of water, the whales quickly get too hot and die. Scientists do not know why whales come ashore.

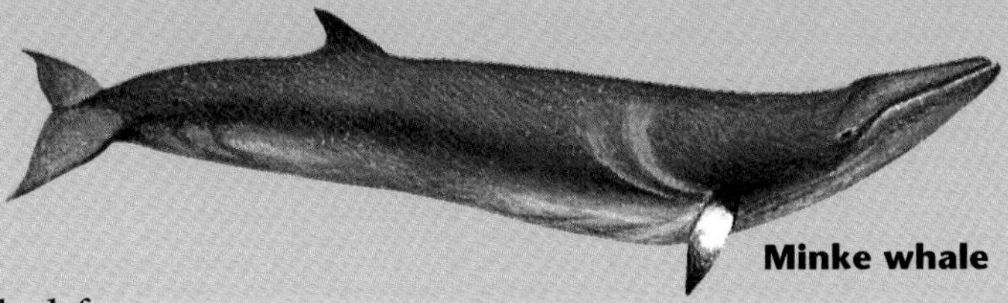

Minke whale

Hunting and saving whales

People have hunted whales for thousands of years. Whales were once killed for their meat and their oil. Whale oil was used as a fuel for lamps and for cooking. Parts of whales were used to make glue, makeup, medicines, soap, and other products. People also ate whale meat.

Narwhal

During the 1900's, whale hunters almost killed off certain kinds of whales. For this reason, groups around the world have worked to protect whales by stopping most whale hunting.

Other articles to read: **Killer whale.**

Beluga

Foods made with wheat are a major part of the diet for over a third of the world's people. Such foods include bread, cake, breakfast cereal, cookies, crackers, and pasta.

Wheat

Wheat is the world's most important food crop. Wheat covers more of the earth's farmland than any other crop. The amount of wheat grown each year could fill a freight train stretching around the world about $2\frac{1}{2}$ times. People eat wheat mainly in bread and other foods made from wheat flour. They eat wheat in macaroni, spaghetti, and other forms of pasta, and in breakfast cereal. Many farm animals eat wheat, too.

Wheat is a kind of grass. Young wheat plants are bright green. The plants grow 2 to 5 feet (0.6 to 1.5 meters) tall and turn golden-brown when ripe.

Each plant has 30 to 50 seeds. The seeds may be red, yellowish-brown, white, purple, or blue. They may be hard or soft. A kind of wheat called durum (*DUR uhm*) wheat has hard seeds. Durum wheat is used in pasta because it holds together well when made into a paste or dough.

To make wheat flour, the wheat seeds are ground up into a fine powder. Whole wheat flour is made from the entire seed. White flour is made from only the soft, white inner part of the seed. White flour does not have the vitamins and minerals found in whole wheat flour. Enriched flour is white flour with added vitamins and minerals.

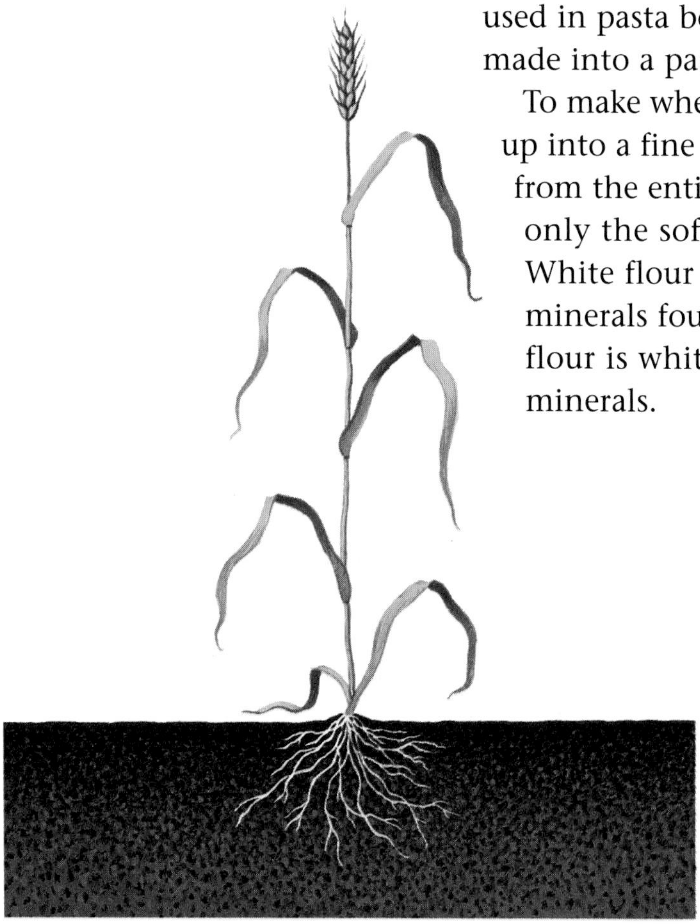

The wheat plant grows up to 5 feet (1.5 meters) high and turns golden-brown when ripe. It holds from 30 to 50 kernels, or seeds, of wheat.

A windlass uses a wheel and axle. This woman uses a windlass to lift water from a well.

Wheel and axle

A wheel and axle is a tool used to lift things. It is made up of a wheel attached to a long rod called an axle. A machine called a windlass uses a wheel and axle. A windlass has one end of a rope attached to an axle. The other end of the rope is attached to the object that needs to be lifted. When someone turns the wheel, the rope winds around the axle and pulls up the object.

A wheel and axle makes lifting easier because the wheel is wider than the axle. As a result, the person turning the wheel does not feel the full weight of the object.

Whippoorwill

The whippoorwill is a bird named for its odd, whistling call. The call sounds like "whip-poor-will, whip-poor-will." The bird lives in forests, mostly in the eastern, central, and southern parts of the United States. The whippoorwill spends the winter along the Gulf Coast, in Mexico, and in Central America.

The whippoorwill is about 10 inches (25 centimeters) long. Its spotted brown feathers make the bird hard to see in the woods. It sleeps in the daytime and feeds at night. Whippoorwills eat insects. Farmers like to have them near their fields because they eat insects that are harmful to crops.

Whippoorwill

White, E. B.

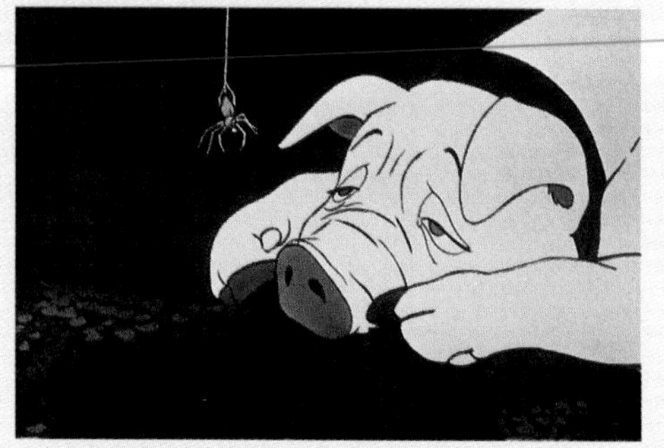

Charlotte's Web, a favorite children's book by E. B. White, is the story of a friendship between a spider and a pig.

E. B. White (1899-1985) was an American author who wrote *Charlotte's Web*. White was known mainly for his short articles and children's books, but he also wrote poetry. Besides *Charlotte's Web* (1952), his children's books are *Stuart Little* (1945) and *The Trumpet of the Swan* (1970). In all these books, the animals talk and act like people.

Elwyn Brooks White was born in Mount Vernon, New York. He spent much of his life in Maine. White started writing for *The New Yorker* magazine in 1925. He wrote about many subjects, including baseball, farming, and marriage. Many of White's works tell of his life in Maine. White won a special Pulitzer Prize in 1978 for his writings.

White House

The White House is the home of the president of the United States. It stands at 1600 Pennsylvania Avenue in Washington, D.C. The White House has 132 rooms. It includes living space for the president's family, offices for the president and staff, a kitchen, a library, the office of the White House doctor, a bowling alley, a swimming pool, and a movie theater. Beautiful gardens surround the White House.

The White House is one of the most popular places to visit in the United States. Every year, more than 1 million visitors go through parts of the home. Most visitors only see the five rooms on the ground floor. These rooms show the beauty of the building.

This view of the White House shows the North Portico, one of the main entrances. Many rooms have been added to each side of the main building.

James Hoban, an Irish-born building planner, created plans for the White House in the late 1700's. President John Adams and his wife, Abigail, were the first people to live in the White House. When British soldiers burned the building on Aug. 24, 1814, during the War of 1812, President James Madison and his wife, Dolley, were forced to leave the White House. In 1817, after it was rebuilt, President James Monroe and his wife, Elizabeth, moved in. Over the years, presidents have added more rooms, beautiful art, and other features to the White House.

Other articles to read: **President of the United States.**

Whitney, Eli

Eli Whitney (*EE ly HWIHT nee*) (1765-1825) was an American inventor who is best known for creating the cotton gin. The cotton gin is a machine that separates cotton seeds from the cotton fibers, the fluffy threads. Whitney's cotton gin could clean as much cotton in one day as 50 people working by hand. The machine quickly helped the United States become the world's leading cotton grower. Whitney also became a maker of guns and other weapons.

Eli Whitney

Whitney was born in Westborough, Massachusetts. Early in his life, he showed a talent for making things. When he was 12 years old, he made a violin. In 1792, Whitney went to Savannah, Georgia, to teach and study law. His friend Catherine Littlefield Greene suggested that he build a machine to clean cotton. By April 1793, he had built the cotton gin.

Other articles to read: **Cotton.**

The cotton gin cleaned the seeds from cotton fibers. A single machine could clean as much cotton in one day as 50 people could clean picking out the seeds by hand.

Powdered wigs are still worn by English judges today.

Wig

A wig is a covering of hair for the head. Some people wear wigs because they are bald. Others wear wigs for fashion. The best wigs have good quality human hair in them. Some wigs are made with a net. The hair of the person wearing the wig can go through the net and mix with the wig's hair.

The custom of wearing wigs dates back thousands of years. Even Egyptian mummies have been found with them. In the 1600's, wigs became large and expensive. They were usually powdered white. In those days, wigs were worn by nobles, judges, doctors, and professional people. English judges still wear them today.

A wig is part of singer Dolly Parton's makeup when she performs.

A wigwam had a frame of poles covered with bark or with mats made of reeds. Wigwams were made by American Indians who lived in the northeastern woodlands.

Wigwam

A wigwam is the name of a tent or house in which certain American Indians lived. Some wigwams were made of light poles tied together with bark. The poles formed an oval-shaped building with a rounded roof. The poles were covered with layers of bark or reed mats, laid in overlapping rows like the shingles on a house roof. Other wigwams were rectangular with a pointed roof, and some were cone-shaped.

Wigwams were used by Algonquian Indians, who lived in what is now the northeastern United States. Many Plains Indians lived in cone-shaped tepees, which were covered with animal skins.

Wilder, Laura Ingalls

Laura Ingalls Wilder (1867-1957) was an American author of books for children. She is best known for her nine "Little House" books, such as *Little House on the Prairie* (1935). These books tell the story of Laura's life growing up in the Midwest in the 1870's and 1880's. They start with her life in her childhood home in the wilderness and end with her final home with her husband, Almanzo Wilder. These gentle, funny stories show the importance of a close family.

Laura Ingalls was born in Pepin, Wisconsin. As a child, she lived a rugged pioneer life. Her family moved from place to place. She married Almanzo Wilder in 1885.

Laura Ingalls Wilder, *standing,* with her sisters Carrie, *left,* and Mary, *center.*

William I, the Conqueror

William I, the Conqueror, (1027?-1087) was king of England from 1066 until 1087. William was born in the area of northwestern France called Normandy. He became ruler of Normandy when he was 8 years old.

William expected to become king of England in 1066, after King Edward of England died. However, King Edward's brother-in-law, Harold, became king instead. William became angry and decided to send his army to conquer, or take over, England. At the same time, the king of Norway sent his forces into northern England. While Harold's army was busy fighting the Norwegians in the north, William's army landed on the southern coast. After William's army killed Harold at the Battle of Hastings on October 14, 1066, William became king. He was a strong leader.

William I, the Conqueror

Williams, Robin

Robin Williams

Robin Williams (1952-) is an American actor and comedian. He is known for his high energy and his funny imitations. Williams received an Academy Award in 1998 for his performance in *Good Will Hunting* (1998).

Williams was born in Chicago. He grew up near Detroit and in San Francisco. Williams performed funny speeches in Los Angeles clubs and on television comedy programs. His first big success came with his character Mork on the TV show "Mork and Mindy," which started in 1978. His movies include *Good Morning, Vietnam* (1987), *Hook* (1991), *Jumanji* (1995), and *Patch Adams* (1998). Williams was also the voice of the genie in the cartoon film *Aladdin* (1992).

Wilson, Woodrow

Woodrow Wilson

Woodrow Wilson (1856-1924) became the twenty-eighth president of the United States in 1913. He led the United States through World War I (1914-1918).

Wilson was probably born on December 29, 1856, at Staunton, Virginia. Historians are not sure about the date. His father taught him much at home. Wilson graduated from Princeton University in 1879. He then worked as a lawyer. Wilson returned to school and graduated from Johns Hopkins University in Baltimore in 1886. Wilson became a professor at Princeton University in 1890.

Wilson was elected president of Princeton in 1902. He ran for governor of New Jersey and won in 1910. Two years later, he was elected president of the United States.

As president, Wilson worked to improve the banking system, shorten the workday, and improve education. In 1916, he was reelected. Wilson called for war against Germany in 1917, after German submarines attacked American ships. He provided much leadership during the war.

After the war, Wilson worked on the peace treaty and helped start the League of Nations. This group was set up to keep world peace. But Congress would not agree to support it, and the United States never joined the League. Wilson had a stroke in 1919 and became paralyzed. In 1920, he was awarded the 1919 Nobel Peace Prize for starting the League of Nations.

Wind

Wind is moving air. Wind may blow so gently that it can hardly be felt. Or it may blow so hard that it smashes buildings, pushes over large trees, or whips up ocean waves that sink ships and flood the land.

Wind is a part of weather. A hot, moist day may suddenly turn cool if a wind blows in from a cool area. Another wind may blow the clouds away and let the sun warm the land again.

The sun helps create wind. When the sun shines, it heats the land and the air. The warmed air is lighter than cool air, so it rises, and cooler air fills its place. This movement of air causes the wind.

Other articles to read: **Cyclone; Dune; Hurricane; Monsoon; Tornado; Windmill.**

Wind is moving air. We can feel the air when it pushes against us.

Windmills use energy from the wind. The older windmill, *front,* pumps water into a pond. The newer wind turbines, *background,* make electric current.

Windmill

A windmill is a machine that works by wind power. Windmills are used mainly to provide power to pump water, grind up grain, or make electric energy.

Most windmills have a wheel made of two or more blades or sails. The blades are attached to a bar called a shaft. The shaft is mounted on a tower, mast, or other tall structure. When the wind blows the blades, it turns the shaft. The shaft then provides the power that runs the water pump, flour mill, or electric generator.

Modern windmills that help make electric energy are often called wind turbines. Wind turbines are becoming an important source of energy.

Winfrey, Oprah

Oprah Winfrey (1954-) is an American TV host and the producer of a popular television talk show. Her TV and film production studio is Harpo Productions. Winfrey is also an actress.

Oprah Winfrey

Oprah Gail Winfrey was born in Kosciusko, Mississippi. She lived with her mother. Her family was poor. Winfrey later moved to Nashville to live with her father. At age 19, while attending Tennessee State University, Winfrey became the first African American woman to host a TV news show in Nashville. Winfrey began hosting a talk show called "A.M. Chicago" in 1984. The show was renamed "The Oprah Winfrey Show" in 1985. Winfrey has won many awards as best talk-show host. In 2000, she helped start *O, The Oprah Magazine,* a magazine for women.

Winnemucca, Sarah

Sarah Winnemucca

Sarah Winnemucca (*wihn uh MUHK uh*) (1844?-1891), was an American Indian leader. She became famous for speaking out about the government's poor treatment of the Indian people. Winnemucca was a member of the Paiute (*py YOOT*) tribe.

Winnemucca was born near Humboldt Sink in what is now Nevada. In the 1870's, she spoke against the government for taking Paiute land and because the United States Army attacked a Paiute settlement.

In 1880, Winnemucca met with President Rutherford B. Hayes to talk about her people. She gave talks on the mistreatment of the Paiute and also wrote a book called *Life Among the Paiutes: Their Claims and Wrongs* (1883). She later started two schools for Paiute children.

Winnipeg

Winnipeg (*WIHN uh pehg*) is the capital of Manitoba, a Canadian province. The city lies about 60 miles (97 kilometers) north of the Canada-United States border between the Red and Assiniboine (*uh SIHN uh boyn*) rivers.

The city lies in a rich farming region where many farmers grow grain. As a result, many grain businesses have their headquarters in Winnipeg. The city is also a transportation center.

American Indians lived in the area for many years. In 1738, Sieur de la Verendrye (*syur duh lah vay RAHN dree*), a French-Canadian fur trader, reached what is now Winnipeg. The area then became a fur-trading center. Winnipeg became the capital of Manitoba in 1870.

Legislative Building and business area, Winnipeg, Manitoba

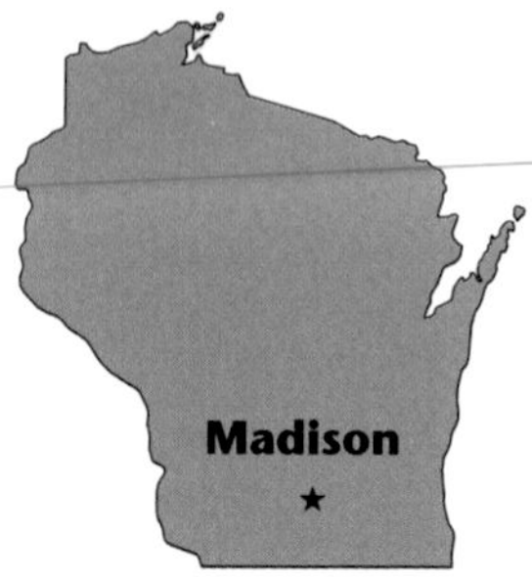

Wisconsin (blue) ranks 26th in size among the states.

State flag

State seal

Wisconsin

Wisconsin (*wihs KAHN suhn*) is a state in the Midwestern region of the United States. Minnesota and Iowa lie to the west, Michigan lies to the north, and Lake Michigan lies to the east. Illinois lies to the south. Lake Superior forms part of Wisconsin's northern border. Much of Wisconsin's western border follows the Mississippi River.

Wisconsin is called the *Badger State.* This nickname comes from Wisconsin's early lead miners. They reminded people of badgers digging holes in the ground.

Madison is the capital and second largest city of Wisconsin. It lies in south-central Wisconsin. Milwaukee is the largest city. It lies in southeast Wisconsin along the shores of Lake Michigan. Milwaukee is an important manufacturing center in the United States and a major Great Lakes port.

Dairy cows on a Wisconsin farm

Land. Wisconsin is a land of hills, plains, valleys, and lakes. Small lakes, hills, and forests cover most of northern Wisconsin. In the middle of the state, the Wisconsin River has cut the Wisconsin Dells, a deep, narrow canyon with steep, rocky sides. Visitors come to the Wisconsin Dells to see its many unusual rock formations. Door County in northeastern Wisconsin also attracts many visitors.

Rolling plains stretch across eastern Wisconsin. The rich soil in this region is good for farming.

Steep slopes and winding ridges give western Wisconsin its beauty. Small cliffs, or bluffs, of limestone and sandstone line the Mississippi River.

Resources and products. Wisconsin farmers raise thousands of milk cows. Wisconsin is one of the nation's leading producers of milk, butter, and cheese.

Farmers also raise beef cattle and hogs. They grow corn, hay, and oats to feed to livestock. Wisconsin grows more green peas, snap beans, and sweet corn than any other state. Beets, cabbages, cucumbers, lima beans, cranberries, apples, raspberries, and strawberries are also major crops.

Wisconsin is a leading state in making machinery, food products, and paper products. Northern Wisconsin has many paper mills.

Important dates in Wisconsin

Indian days	The Dakota, Menominee, and Winnebago Indians lived in the Wisconsin region before European people arrived.
1634	Jean Nicolet, a French explorer, landed on the Green Bay shore.
1673	Explorers Louis Jolliet of Canada and Father Jacques Marquette of France traveled through the region.
1763	England took control of the region from France.
1783	The Wisconsin region became part of the United States.
1836	Congress created the Wisconsin Territory.
1848	Wisconsin became the 30th U.S. state on May 29.
1867	Frank Lloyd Wright, one of America's most important architects, was born in Richland Center.
1870's	The dairy industry began in Wisconsin. This industry remains Wisconsin's most important type of farming.
1871	About 1,200 people were killed in a forest fire that destroyed Peshtigo and nearby villages.
1948	Wisconsin marked its centennial, or 100th anniversary, as a U.S. state.
1967	The Green Bay Packers, Wisconsin's football team, won the first Super Bowl game.
1987	Tommy G. Thompson was elected governor of Wisconsin. He served for more than 10 years, longer than any other governor in Wisconsin's history.

The first kindergarten in the United States was opened in 1856 in Watertown.

Other articles to read: **Marquette, Jacques; Wright, Frank Lloyd.**

Facts About Wisconsin

Capital: Madison.

Area: 56,145 sq. mi. (145,414 km^2).

Population: 5,363,675.

Year of statehood: 1848.

State abbreviations: Wis. (traditional), WI (postal).

State motto: *Forward.*

State song: "On, Wisconsin!" Words by J. S. Hubbard and Charles D. Rosa; music by William T. Purdy.

Largest cities: Milwaukee, Madison, Green Bay.

Government:

State government:
Governor: 4-year term.
State senators: 33; 4-year terms.
State representatives: 99; 2-year terms.
Counties: 72.

Federal government:
U.S. senators: 2.
U.S. representatives: 8.
Electoral votes: 10.

State bird
Robin

State flower
Wood violet

Wisterias are often used to cover outside walls or archways.

Wisteria

Wisteria (*wihs TIHR ee uh*) is the name of a group of thick-growing vines that produce large bunches of drooping flowers. The flowers may be light bluish-purple, pink, or white. The plant grows in China and the eastern United States.

Wisterias are climbing vines that may grow more than 35 feet (11 meters) tall. They are often used to cover outside walls or archways. Wisterias grow well in deep soil with plenty of moisture. Wisteria pods and seeds contain a poison that can cause serious stomach problems if eaten. Wisterias belong to the pea family.

Witch. See **Witchcraft.**

Witchcraft

People were accused of being witches during trials held in Salem, Massachusetts, in 1692. Nineteen people were hanged as witches.

Witchcraft is supposedly a kind of magic power. In many parts of the world, people have believed in witchcraft for hundreds of years. Some people still use witchcraft today. A woman or man who uses witchcraft is called a witch. In the past, male witches were also called warlocks or wizards. Some people believe that witches can fly and can control spirits and the weather. Other people do not believe in witches at all.

Throughout history, people have thought that witchcraft is evil. People have also believed that witches use their magic to cause bad luck, accidents, sickness, or even death. However, some people believe that witches also use their magic to help others.

Witness

A witness is a person who speaks in a court of law after promising to tell "the truth, the whole truth, and nothing but the truth." The promise made by a witness is called an oath (*ohth*). Witnesses then give testimony (*TEHS tuh moh nee*)—they say what they know about the case. They may answer questions from a judge or from lawyers. A witness who lies after taking the oath is guilty of a crime called perjury (*PUR juh ree*) and may be punished.

A witness may also be a person who signs a legal paper, such as a will. The signature shows that the person watched the will being signed.

A witness takes an oath to tell the truth before giving testimony in court.

Wolf

A wolf is a wild animal and one of the largest members of the dog family. It looks like a large German shepherd dog, but a wolf has longer legs, bigger feet, a wider head, and a long, bushy tail. Wolves are good hunters because they can see, hear, and smell very well. A wolf can see and smell a deer more than 1 mile (1.6 kilometers) away. Wolves eat almost any animal that they can catch.

Many people are afraid of wolves. The howl of these animals frightens people, and some people believe wolves attack human beings. Such stories as "Little Red Riding Hood," in which a wolf eats a little girl's grandmother, also give the wrong idea about wolves. The truth is that wolves stay away from people as much as possible.

Almost all wolves belong to a species (*SPEESH eez*), or kind, called the gray wolf. The two main

Wolf

A **wolf's fur** can be brown, gray, a mixture of brown and gray, or even black. Arctic wolves have pale coats that blend with the snow, so that they are hard to see.

types of gray wolves are the timber wolf and the tundra wolf. The timber wolf lives in the forests of northern Asia, Europe, and North America. The fur of most timber wolves is brown, gray, or a mixture of those colors. A few have black fur. The tundra wolf, also called the Arctic wolf or white wolf, has white fur and lives in the far north Arctic region. Another kind of wolf, the red wolf, has almost died out. Only a few hundred red wolves are still alive, mostly in zoos or animal parks.

Wollstonecraft, Mary

Mary Wollstonecraft (*WUL stuhn kraft*) (1759-1797) was a British writer. She was best known for her book *A Vindication of the Rights of Woman,* which she wrote in 1792. This book was one of the first to say that women should be equal to men. At that time, many people thought women were not as smart as men. Wollstonecraft pointed out that girls got much less education than boys did. Sometimes, they got no schooling at all. Wollstonecraft wrote that girls and women should get a better education.

Mary Wollstonecraft

Wollstonecraft was born in London. She died 11 days after her daughter, Mary Wollstonecraft Shelley, was born. Shelley wrote the famous book *Frankenstein* in 1818.

Wolverine

A wolverine (*WUL vuh REEN*) is an animal that looks somewhat like a small bear. It has a heavy body and short legs. It has dark brown or black fur with a band of lighter-colored fur along its sides to the top of its bushy tail. Adult wolverines are about $3\frac{1}{2}$ feet (110 centimeters) long and weigh up to 55 pounds (25 kilograms). They are powerful for their size. Wolverines live in northern parts of North America, Europe, and Asia.

In summer, wolverines eat small animals, birds, and plants. In winter, they hunt reindeer and caribou. They tear the body apart and hide the pieces to eat later.

Wolverine

Wonder, Stevie

Stevie Wonder (1950-) is an American musician. He writes songs, sings, and plays keyboard instruments. His music includes fast songs with Jamaican and African beats and slow songs about love. In 1984, Wonder won an Academy Award for his song "I Just Called to Say I Love You" from the movie *The Woman in Red.* In 1989, he was elected to the Rock and Roll Hall of Fame.

Wonder was born in Saginaw, Michigan. His real name is Stevland Morris. Wonder has been blind since he was a baby. He was 13 years old when he recorded his first hit song, "Fingertips," in 1963. His many other hits include "Superstition" (1972), "You Are the Sunshine of My Life" (1973), and "Sir Duke" (1977). He also sang "True to Your Heart" in the movie *Mulan* (1998).

Stevie Wonder

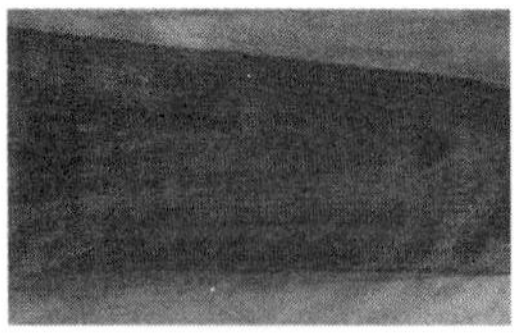
Birch

Cherry

Mahogany

Maple

Rosewood

Sycamore

Some types of hardwoods

Wood

Wood is a tough substance under the bark of trees, shrubs, and some other plants. Wood is used to make thousands of products, including baseball bats, floors, furniture, musical instruments, paper, and even rayon cloth. Wood is a good building material because it is strong and easy to handle. Wood does not rust, and it stands up to high heat better than steel does.

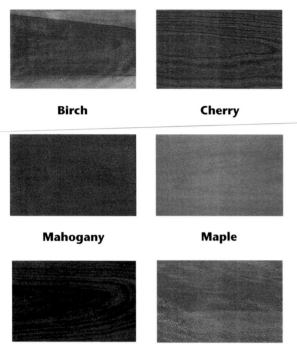

The two main kinds of wood are hardwood and softwood. Hardwood comes from trees with broad leaves, including birch, cherry, elm, mahogany, maple, and oak. Softwood comes from trees with cones, including cedar, Douglas-fir, pine, redwood, and spruce. Softwood is easy to saw, but it is not really soft.

Woodchuck

Woodchucks, also called ground hogs, are small animals that belong to the squirrel family. Woodchucks live in Canada and in the eastern and midwestern United States.

There are several kinds of woodchucks. The woodchuck of Canada and the eastern United States is about 2 feet (61 centimenters) long, including its bushy tail. It has a broad, flat head, grayish-brown fur on the upper parts of its body, and yellowish-brown fur on its underparts.

Woodchucks eat alfalfa, clover, and other plants. They dig tunnels underground to make their homes, called burrows or dens. Woodchucks hibernate, or sleep a long time, over the winter.

According to a tradition, if a woodchuck sees its shadow on February 2, called Ground-Hog Day, there will be six more weeks of winter. If it does not see its shadow, spring will come soon.

Woodpecker

A woodpecker is a bird that uses its long, sharp bill for drilling into trees. Woodpeckers poke holes in bark and wood to find insects to eat. They also dig holes in the trunks of trees to make a nest.

Woodpeckers live in almost every part of the world. Their homes range from evergreen forests to deserts. There are about 200 kinds of woodpeckers. The redheaded woodpecker of the eastern and central United States has a bright-red head and neck. The black woodpecker is the largest European woodpecker. The great slaty woodpecker is a large Asian kind. The cardinal woodpecker is the most common kind in Africa, south of the Sahara Desert.

Some kinds of woodpeckers

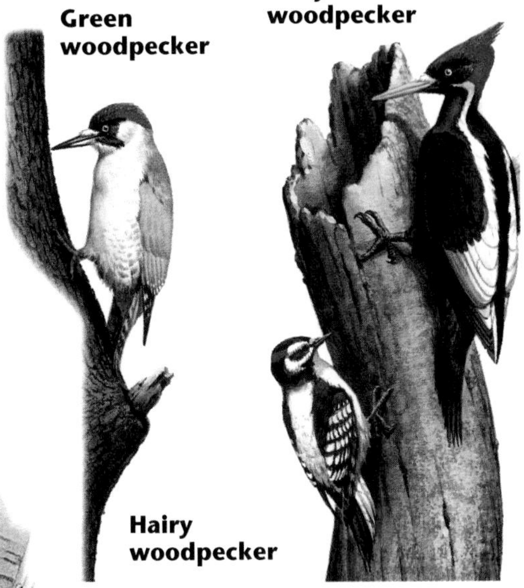

A woodpecker drills a hole into a tree with its beak, then scoops outs insects with its long, spiky tongue.

Woods, Tiger

Tiger Woods (1975-   ) is an American golfer. In 2000, Woods became the youngest golfer to complete a Grand Slam. The Grand Slam of golf consists of the United States Open, the British Open, and the Professional Golfers' Association (PGA) Championship.

Woods turned professional in 1996 and won two pro tournaments that year. In 1997, at age 21, he became the youngest golfer and the first with African American heritage to win the Masters Tournament. He won the Masters again in 2001, 2002, and 2005; the PGA Championship in 1999 and 2000; the U.S. Open in 2000 and 2002; and the British Open in 2000 and 2005.

Woods was born in Cypress, California. His real name is Eldrick Woods. His background is African American, American Indian, Chinese, European, and Thai.

Tiger Woods

Woodson, Carter Godwin

Carter Godwin Woodson

Carter Godwin Woodson (1875-1950) was an American author who wrote about the history of black people. Woodson wrote 16 books and many magazine stories. Woodson's best-known book is *Negro in Our History,* which he wrote in 1922. In Woodson's time, a black person was called a Negro.

Woodson was born in New Canton, Virginia. His parents had been slaves. He went to college at Harvard University, where he studied history. In 1915, Woodson established the Association for the Study of Negro Life and History. This organization produced a magazine called the *Journal of Negro History.* Woodson won the Spingarn Medal in 1926 for his outstanding work.

Some woodwind instruments

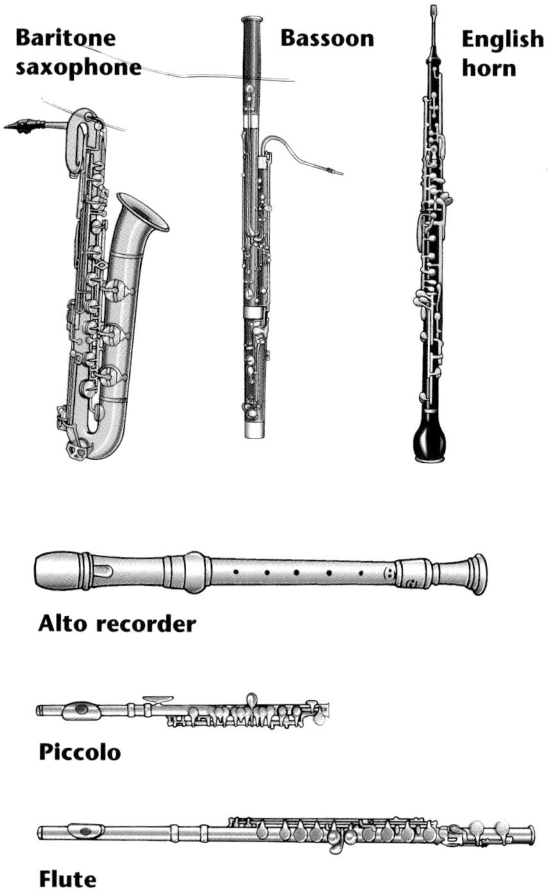

Woodwind instruments

Woodwind instruments are musical instruments that are played by blowing air through a tube. They include the recorder, flute, piccolo, clarinet, oboe, English horn, bassoon, and saxophone. In the past, all woodwind instruments except the saxophone were made of wood. Today, many woodwinds are made of metal, plastic, or other materials. Most orchestras and bands have a woodwind section.

In such woodwinds as recorders, the player blows through a mouthpiece into the instrument. In some other woodwinds, such as flutes and piccolos, the player blows across a hole in the instrument.

Still other woodwinds, called reed instruments, have one or two reeds attached to the mouthpiece. A reed is a thin strip of wood, metal, or plastic. It vibrates—moves quickly back and forth—when the musician blows on it. The clarinet and saxophone are the most popular single-reed instruments. Double-reed instruments include the bassoon, English horn, and oboe.

On all woodwind instruments, the player produces different notes by placing his or her fingers over holes in the instrument or on keys that cover the holes. When all the holes are covered, the air that the player blows into the instrument goes straight through and out the end. But when one or more holes are left open, some of the air goes out the holes, and so the sound is different. Each note is the result of a certain combination of open and closed holes.

Wool

Wool is the soft, curly hair of sheep and some other animals. People spin wool into yarn and use it to make clothing, blankets, and rugs. Wool cloth is easy to clean, does not wrinkle easily, and holds its shape well. Wool is especially popular for coats, sweaters, gloves, and socks, because it keeps out the cold so well.

Almost all wool comes from sheep. There are five basic kinds of wool. They are fine wool, crossbred wool, medium wool, long wool, and coarse wool. Different kinds of wool come from different kinds of fleece, or sheep's hair.

Fine wool is used to make the best clothing. Crossbred wool is used for outdoor clothing. Medium wool is used to make cloth coverings for furniture. Long wool is used to make carpets and heavy cloth. Coarse wool is used

Wool cloth is made in several steps. First, the fleece is sheared from a sheep.

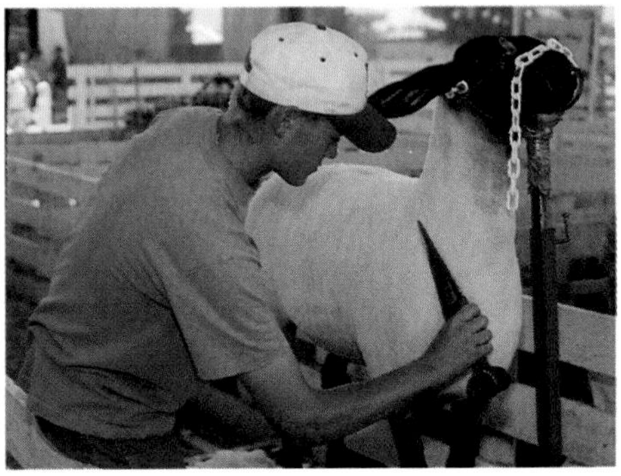

The wool is untangled and arranged into a sheet by carding machines.

The wool is woven into fabric by power looms.

A worker checks a large power loom that is used to weave wool cloth.

for carpets and craft yarns. Some wool also comes from goats, camels, alpacas, and vicuñas.

In most parts of the world, farmers shear their sheep, or cut off the wool, once a year. Cutting the wool does not hurt the sheep, and they soon grow a new coat. The wool is spun into yarn and made into cloth in factories. Australia, New Zealand, and China are the world's top wool producers.

Other articles to read: **Knitting; Weaving.**

Word processing

Word processing means using a computer to type, change, and print letters, reports, and other written documents. Many people today use computers instead of typewriters.

Personal computers need special instructions called programs or software to be able to do word processing. The letters and numbers are shown on a computer screen as the user types them. The typed material can be easily changed or moved. Most word processing programs allow the writer to check for spelling errors. Many can also find some mistakes in the writer's grammar.

At the touch of a key, the writer can print out an entire document. The computer can also store the document, so that the writer can easily make changes or new copies later.

Many people today use computers instead of typewriters.

World. See Earth.

World War I

World War I was a long and terrible war. It began on June 28, 1914, and ended on November 11, 1918. Never before had so many nations been involved in one war. Nearly 10 million soldiers died during the four years of the war. Most of the battles took place in Europe. They were fought on land, at sea, and in the air.

The war was called the Great War until another world war started in 1939. Then the Great War became known as World War I, and the second world war was called World War II.

Two groups of nations fought World War I. One group was called the Central Powers. It included Germany, Austria-Hungary, Bulgaria, and the Ottoman Empire. The other group was called the Allies. It was made up of more than 20 countries. The main Allied powers were France, Britain, Russia, and the United States.

Air power became important during World War I. Pilots for the Allies and the Central Powers fought battles in the air over Europe.

New weapons used in World War I

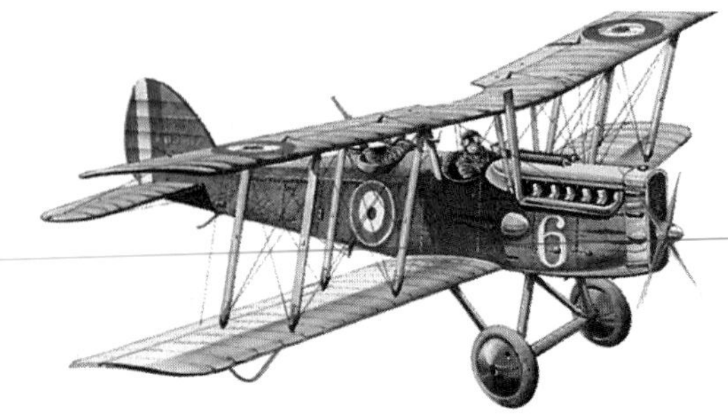

Airplane

Tank

Submarine

Machine gun

There were many reasons for World War I. But the event that started the war was the assassination, or killing, of Archduke Franz Ferdinand, the ruler of a country called Austria-Hungary. The man who killed the archduke, Gavrilo Princip, was connected with a terrorist group in the country of Serbia. Leaders in Austria-Hungary believed that Serbia's government had ordered the killing, so Austria-Hungary called for war against Serbia.

After the fighting began, France and Russia took Serbia's side and became the Allies. Germany took Austria-Hungary's side, and the two nations became the Central Powers. As the war continued, other nations joined on one side or the other. Britain joined the Allies two months after France and Russia. The United States entered the war on April 6, 1917, on the side of the Allies. The U.S. forces gave the Allies the extra power they needed to win the war.

After the Central Powers surrendered, or gave up, a peace treaty was signed. Austria-Hungary and Germany gave up some of their land, and the names and borders of some countries changed. However, the peace lasted for only about 20 years, and then World War II began.

Several new kinds of weapons and warfare were introduced during World War I. Germany used poison gas in 1915. Another new weapon was the flame thrower, which shot out a stream of burning fuel. Troops on both sides used machine guns to kill enemy soldiers who were running toward them. The British introduced the tank in 1916. The airplane, which had been invented in 1903, was first used in battle during World War I. Air battles were called dogfights. The submarine had also been invented long before World War I, but the Germans were the first to use submarines effectively as deadly warships.

Other articles to read: **Airplane; Submarine; Tank; Unknown soldier; Wilson, Woodrow.**

World War II

World War II killed more people and destroyed more property than any other war in history. It began on September 1, 1939, and ended on September 2, 1945. World War II began in Europe but spread to nearly every part of the world, including northern Africa, Asia, Australia, and the Pacific Ocean. Battles were fought on land, at sea, and in the air.

About 17 million soldiers died during the six years of the war. An even greater number of men, women, and children also died from bombs, sickness, or lack of food. Millions of people died as prisoners in Germany's death camps. The war left many other people without homes or jobs.

Two groups of nations fought World War II. One group, called the Axis, was made up of nine countries and was led by Germany, Italy, and Japan. The other group, called the Allies, was made up of 50 countries and was led by Britain, China, the Soviet Union, and the United States.

There were many reasons for World War II. The war was caused in part by problems that were left over from World War I (1914-1918). World War II actually began when troops from Germany entered Poland on September 1, 1939. Adolf Hitler, the leader of Germany, wanted more land for his country, so he decided to take land away from Poland. Two days later, Britain, France, and several other nations joined Poland in the war against Germany. German troops moved on into other parts of Europe, taking over land and making enemies.

The biggest sea battles of World War II took place between airplanes and ships.

As the war continued, many other nations joined one side or the other. Before the war, the Soviet Union and Germany had made an agreement not to fight each other. However, German forces later attacked the Soviet Union, which then joined the Allies against Germany. The United States entered World War II after Japanese warplanes attacked Pearl Harbor, a U.S. Navy base in Hawaii, on December 7, 1941.

Early in the war, Germany won many battles in Europe. But after the Soviet Union and the United States joined the Allies, German troops began to lose more battles. Allied forces made a big attack on the German troops in Europe on June 6, 1944, a date nicknamed D-Day. Germany finally surrendered, or gave up, on May 7, 1945.

But Japan kept on fighting. To make Japan give up, the United States dropped two atomic bombs on Japanese cities in August 1945. Japan surrendered on September 2, 1945, and World War II ended at last.

Other articles to read: **D-Day; Frank, Anne; Holocaust; Pearl Harbor Naval Base; Unknown soldier.**

Important weapons of World War II included bombers and fighter planes, trucks that carried people and supplies over land and water, tanks, and aircraft carriers.

World Wide Web. See **Internet.**

World's fair

A world's fair is a show in which many nations exhibit their arts, crafts, inventions, foods, and other products. Most world's fairs also have entertainment and fun things for people to do.

A world's fair runs for several months, and millions of people come to visit the fair. Most fairs have been held in Europe and the United States. But some have been held in Africa, Australia, Canada, India, Japan, and New Zealand.

The first world's fair was the Great Exhibition of 1851 held in the Crystal Palace in London. In 1992, a world's fair was held in Seville, Spain. The Bureau of International Expositions makes the rules for world's fairs.

The first world's fair was held in the Crystal Palace, London, in 1851.

Worm

A worm is an animal that has a soft, thin body and no backbone or legs. There are thousands of kinds of worms. The largest kinds grow many feet or meters long, and the smallest ones cannot be seen without a microscope.

Some worms live in water or soil. Many of those worms eat small plants and animals. Other worms live in plants or inside the bodies of certain animals. These worms are parasites (*PAR uh syts*), living things that feed off the plant or animal they live on or in. They sometimes make the plant or animal they live in, called the host, sick.

Most kinds of worms have a well-developed sense of touch. Many have a sense of sight, with eyes or eyespots on the head.

There are four main groups of worms: flatworms, ribbon worms, roundworms, and segmented worms. Flatworms are the simplest kinds of worms. They

Earthworm (segmented worm)

Leech

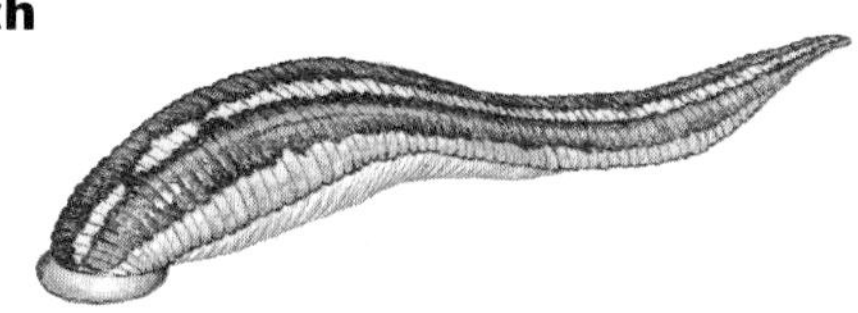

Ragworm

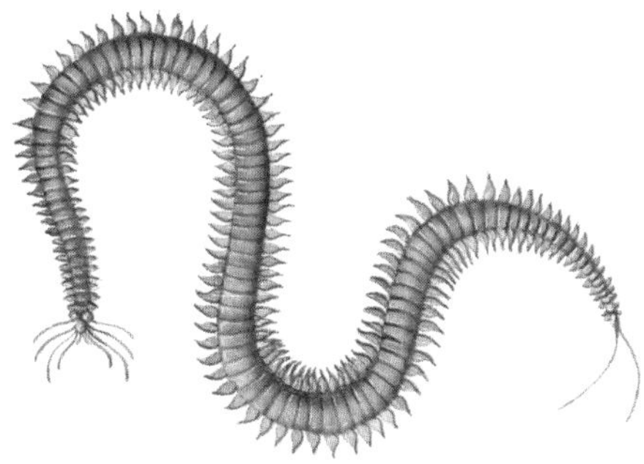

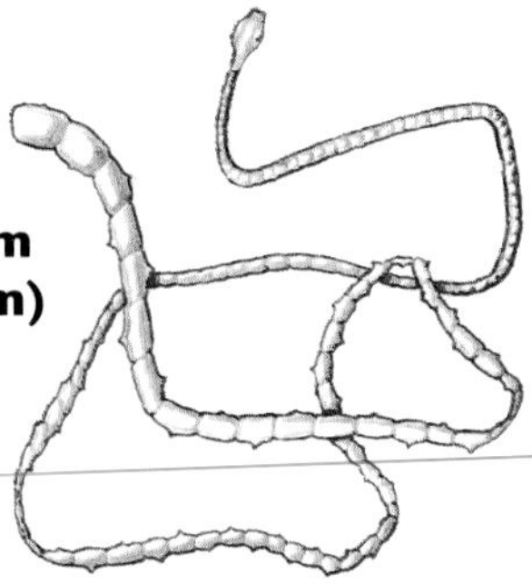
Tapeworm (flatworm)

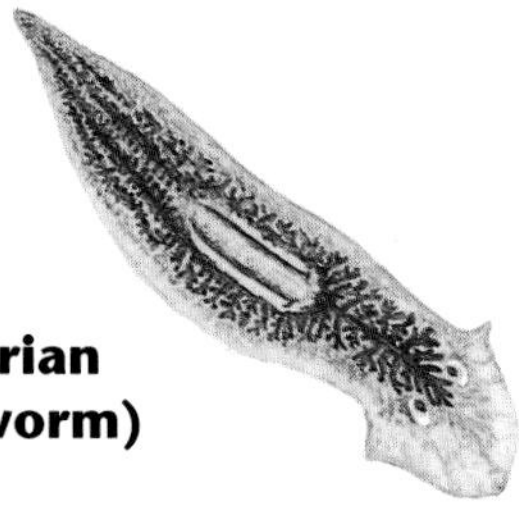
Planarian (flatworm)

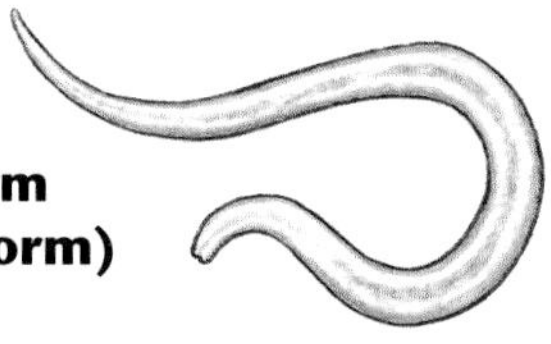
Hookworm (roundworm)

include planarians, which live in ponds and lakes, and tapeworms and flukes, which are parasites. Ribbon worms look somewhat like flatworms, but many are larger, and most live in the sea. Roundworms have a long, tube-shaped body that looks like a piece of thread. Some kinds of roundworms are tiny parasites. Segmented worms, the most highly developed kind of worm, look as if they have rings around their bodies. They include earthworms and leeches. They usually live in water or underground. Some people believe that caterpillars and grubs are worms, but they are really insects.

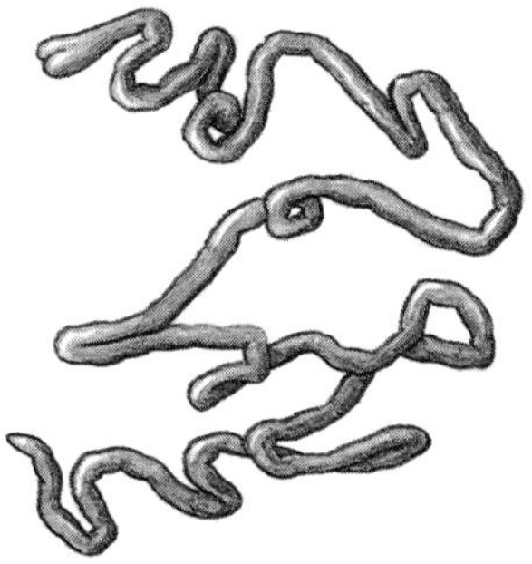
Bootlace worm (ribbon worm)

Other articles to read: **Tapeworm**.

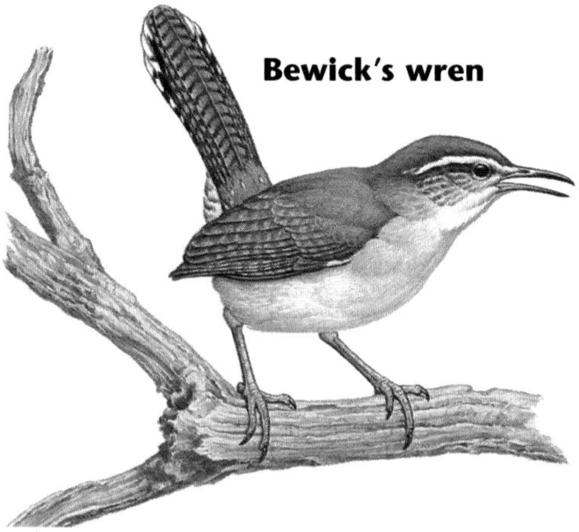
Bewick's wren

Winter wren

Wren

Wrens are small, active birds that live in most parts of the world. A wren has a slender bill and rounded wings. Most wrens are brown and may be striped, spotted, or streaked with black and white. Wrens have short tails that they often hold upward. Wrens eat insects and seeds. They guard their nests carefully.

There are about 60 kinds of wrens in the world. Most live in Asia and the Americas. Only one kind, the common wren, or jenny wren, lives in Europe. It also lives in North America. Wrens of the United States also include the Bewick's wren, cactus wren, and winter wren. Fairywrens live in Australia.

Wrestling

Wrestling is a sport in which two people try to pin, or hold, each other's shoulders to the floor. A wrestler uses movements called holds to grab the opponent and control that person's movements.

There are more than 50 kinds of wrestling, each with its own rules. Nearly all wrestlers are men or boys. Women may wrestle with each other in a kind of wrestling called freestyle. Men also wrestle each other freestyle.

Amateur wrestling

Amateur wrestling is popular in schools in the United States and Canada. Every year, students in elementary school through college take part in wrestling matches. The national and world championship contests are held each year. Every four years, the best wrestlers from around the world take part in the Summer Olympic Games.

The two most popular forms of wrestling in the world are freestyle and Greco-Roman. These two forms of wrestling are much alike. The main difference between the two is how the legs are used. Freestyle wrestlers use their legs to grab, trip, or tackle an opponent. In Greco-Roman wrestling, the legs are used only for support.

Freestyle, the older of the two types, is the more popular form in the United States and Canada. Greco-Roman wrestling is the more popular form throughout Europe. International matches, including the Olympics, have both freestyle and Greco-Roman contests. In both forms, wrestlers are divided into pairs based on how much they weigh.

Some holds and moves in college wrestling

Beginning the match, wrestlers approach each other.

Wrestlers start the second or third period.

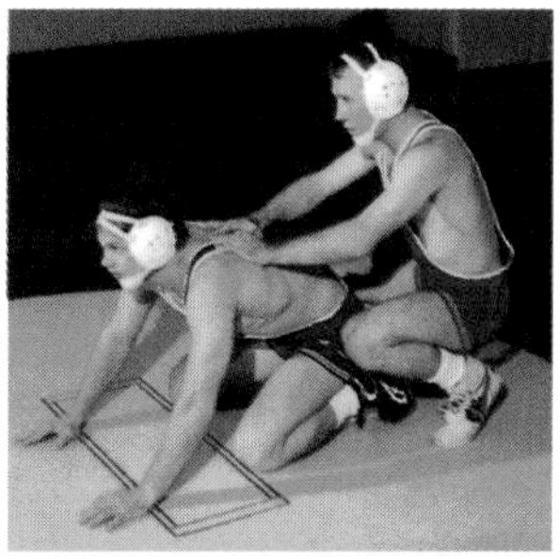

Sometimes wrestlers start another way.

A take down gives a wrestler points.

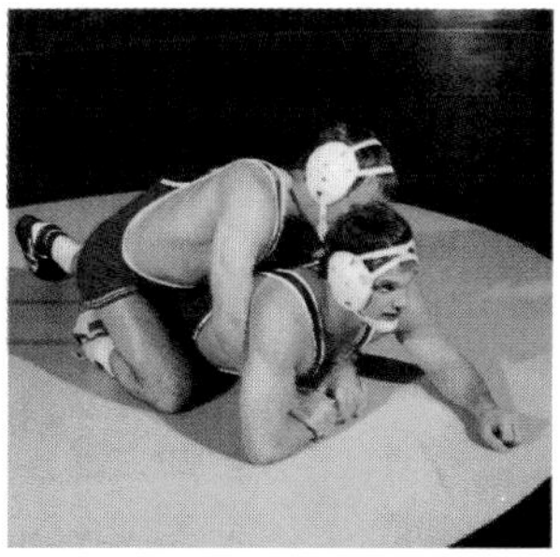

A ride gives the top wrestler control.

An escape sets the bottom wrestler free.

A near fall almost pins the bottom wrestler.

A fall pins the bottom wrestler down and ends the match.

Sumo wrestlers compete in Japan. The wrestlers try to throw each other or push each other out of a marked circle.

International matches have 10 weight classes, or groups.

Other kinds of wrestling

In Japan, the most popular form of wrestling is called sumo (*SOO moh*). Sumo wrestlers, who can weigh over 300 pounds (136 kilograms), try to throw each other to the ground or force the opponent outside a marked circle.

Professional wrestling is popular on TV. It has become more of an entertainment show than a sport. Most matches take place in a roped and padded ring that looks like a boxing ring. Many pro wrestlers wear unusual costumes.

Wilbur and Orville Wright

Wright brothers

The Wright brothers, Wilbur (1867-1912) and Orville (1871-1948), invented and built the first successful airplane. On December 17, 1903, near Kitty Hawk, North Carolina, they made the world's first flight in a heavier-than-air machine. Orville flew the plane 120 feet (37 meters), less than half the length of a football field. The plane stayed in the air 12 seconds and reached a speed of about 30 miles (48 kilometers) per hour, about as fast as a modern car drives along a neighborhood street.

The brothers made three more flights that day. The longest, by Wilbur, was 852 feet (260 meters), almost the length of three football fields, and lasted 59 seconds. Four men and one boy saw the Wrights' first flights, but newspapers were not interested in the story, and TV had not been invented yet. As a result, few people knew what the brothers had done until years later.

The Wrights continued their experiments at a field near their hometown of Dayton, Ohio, in

1904 and 1905. In 1909, the Wrights established a company to build airplanes. Wilbur died of typhoid fever in 1912. Orville sold the company in 1915 but kept doing research on airplanes for the rest of his life.

Wilbur was born on a farm near New Castle, Indiana. Orville was born in Dayton, Ohio. The plane they flew near Kitty Hawk is now in the National Air and Space Museum in Washington, D.C.

The first airplane flight took place near Kitty Hawk, North Carolina, in 1903. It lasted 12 seconds.

Other articles to read: **Airplane.**

Wright, Frank Lloyd

Frank Lloyd Wright (1867-1959) was an important American architect (*AHR kuh tehkt*). An architect designs, or plans, buildings. Over a period of nearly 70 years, Wright created many exciting forms of architecture. Some later architects borrowed ideas from Wright in developing their own styles.

Wright was born in Richland Center, Wisconsin. In 1887, he moved to Chicago. Wright's first important buildings were long, low houses designed in his famous prairie style.

He designed a hotel in Tokyo able to withstand a 1923 earthquake that damaged other buildings. In his final years, he designed the Guggenheim Museum in New York City and the Marin County Civic Center near San Francisco.

"Fallingwater" house, one of Frank Lloyd Wright's best known houses, is built out over a waterfall near Uniontown, Pennsylvania.

Wright, Richard

Richard Wright

Richard Wright (1908-1960) is often thought to be the most important African American writer of his time. Wright was born near Natchez, Mississippi. He became well known as a result of four books he wrote early in his career. These books were the story collection *Uncle Tom's Children* (1938), the novel *Native Son* (1940), the history book *12 Million Black Voices* (1941), and the autobiography *Black Boy* (1945), which tells about his early life. Each book deals with the unfair treatment of black people in American society.

Wright also wrote poetry and articles about his ideas and experiences. His book *White Man, Listen!* (1957) contains some of his short articles.

Writing

Writing is a way of using letters, words, numbers, symbols, or signs to show ideas. Today, most people use some sort of alphabet to write words.

The first step in the development of writing came when early people learned to draw pictures to stand for ideas. Such pictures are called ideographs (*IHD ee uh grafs*). For example, a picture of a smiling face stands for the idea of being happy. People understand the idea of such a picture, no matter what language they speak.

The next step, and the first real writing, came about 5,000 to 5,500 years ago. People learned to show ideas by using signs or symbols to stand for the words of their own language. Such signs are called logographs (*LAWG uh grafs*), and this kind of writing is called logography (*loh GAHG ruh fee*).

The first people to use logography were the Sumerians. They lived in southern Mesopotamia,

Sumerians invented cuneiform writing about 5,000 years ago. Children learned to write by using a tool to make wedge-shaped marks in clay tablets.

a region between the Tigris and Euphrates rivers in what is now the Middle East. They used logography to keep track of who owned certain animals. For example, if a man owned five cows, the Sumerians would write one sign for the number *five,* one sign for the word *cow,* and one sign for the owner's name. Over time, the Sumerians found that they could also use the sign for an object that was easy to draw to stand for a word that sounded the same but was hard to make a picture of.

The Egyptians developed a similar system, called hieroglyphic (*HY uhr uh GLIHF ihk*) writing, about 5,000 years ago. About 3,500 years ago, the Chinese began an advanced word writing system.

About 3,000 to 3,500 years ago, the Phoenicians worked out the earliest alphabets, based on the Egyptian system. The alphabet letters stood for certain sounds. The ancient Greeks borrowed the Phoenician symbols and added vowel signs. The ancient Romans learned the Greek alphabet and made their own letters. Those letters looked much the same as the letters used today in English and some other languages.

Other articles to read: **Alphabet; Egypt, Ancient; Handwriting; Hieroglyphics.**

Wyoming

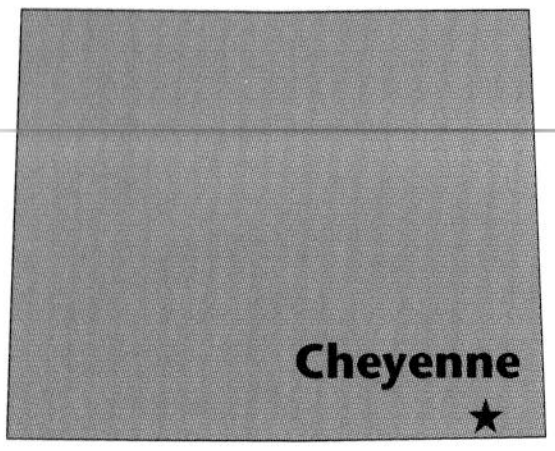

Wyoming (blue) ranks ninth in size among the states.

State flag

State seal

Wyoming is a state in the Rocky Mountain region of the United States. Idaho lies to the west and South Dakota and Nebraska lie to the east. Wyoming is called the *Equality State* because women in Wyoming were the first in the nation to vote, hold public office, and serve on juries.

Cheyenne *(SHY ehn or shy AN),* Wyoming's capital and largest city, is a major trade center. The Continental Divide winds through Wyoming. On the east side of the divide, rivers flow to the Atlantic Ocean. On the west side, rivers flow to the Pacific Ocean.

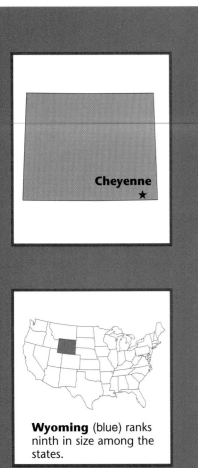

The Teton Mountains rise sharply from a beautiful valley called Jackson Hole in northwestern Wyoming.

Land. Wyoming is famous for its beautiful mountains. The Rocky Mountains sweep across the state in huge ranges. Yellowstone National Park is in the northwest. A famous geyser called Old Faithful is there. It regularly shoots up hot water from below the earth.

The Teton Mountains are among Wyoming's most famous mountains. The Bighorn and Laramie ranges are famous, too.

Wyoming has some flat, dry areas called basins between the mountain ranges. Some basins have rugged towers of rock called buttes *(byoots).*

The Rocky Mountains end in the southeast corner of Wyoming. From there, the Great Plains begins to stretch eastward across the middle of the United States.

Resources and products. Almost all products made in Wyoming come from the land. The most important products, oil and natural gas, come from underground fields. Coal is also mined.

About half of Wyoming's land is used for ranches and farms. Beef cattle, milk, sheep, and wool are the most important farm products. Some farmers also grow sugar beets, hay, wheat, barley, beans, and corn.

Important dates in Wyoming

Indian days	Arapaho, Blackfeet, and Ute Indians were among the many peoples that lived in the area before Europeans arrived.
1807	American fur trapper John Colter explored the Yellowstone area.
1812	A group of American fur trappers led by Robert Stuart discovered South Pass across the Rocky Mountains. This route became important in pioneer travel to the West.
1834	Traders William Sublette and Robert Campbell established Fort William (later Fort Laramie).
1867	The Union Pacific Railroad entered Wyoming.
1868	Congress created the Territory of Wyoming.
1869	The Wyoming territorial government gave women the right to vote, hold office in government, and serve on juries. This law was the first of its kind in the United States.
1872	Yellowstone became the first national park.
1883	Wyoming's first oil well was drilled in the Dallas Field. Oil became one of Wyoming's major products.
1890	Wyoming became the 44th state on July 10.
1906	President Theodore Roosevelt made Devils Tower the first national monument.
1925	Nellie Tayloe Ross was elected governor of Wyoming. She became the first woman governor in the United States.
1960's	The U.S. government began setting up many nuclear weapons in Wyoming.
1988	Fires damaged large areas of Yellowstone National Park.

Yellowstone became the first national park in 1872. John Colter explored the area in 1807.

Other articles to read: **Indian wars; Indian, American; Oregon Trail; Rocky Mountains; Yellowstone National Park.**

Facts About Wyoming

Capital: Cheyenne.

Area: 97,818 sq. mi. (253,349 km²).

Population: 493,782.

Year of statehood: 1890.

State abbreviations: Wyo. (traditional), WY (postal).

State motto: *Equal Rights.*

State song: "Wyoming." Words by Charles E. Winter; music by G. E. Knapp.

Largest cities: Cheyenne, Casper, Laramie.

Government:

State government:

Governor: 4-year term.
State senators: 30; 4-year terms.
State representatives: 60; 2-year terms.
Counties: 23.

Federal government:

U.S. senators: 2.
U.S. representatives: 1.
Electoral votes: 3.

State bird
Meadowlark

State flower
Indian paintbrush

Xx is the twenty-fourth letter of the English alphabet.

Special ways of expressing the letter X

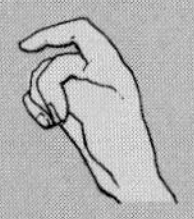

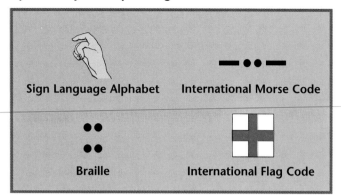

Sign Language Alphabet

— • • —

International Morse Code

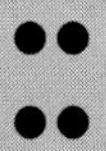

Braille

International Flag Code

Development of the letter X

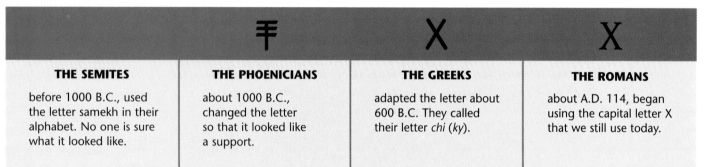

		X	X
THE SEMITES	**THE PHOENICIANS**	**THE GREEKS**	**THE ROMANS**
before 1000 B.C., used the letter samekh in their alphabet. No one is sure what it looked like.	about 1000 B.C., changed the letter so that it looked like a support.	adapted the letter about 600 B.C. They called their letter *chi* (*ky*).	about A.D. 114, began using the capital letter X that we still use today.

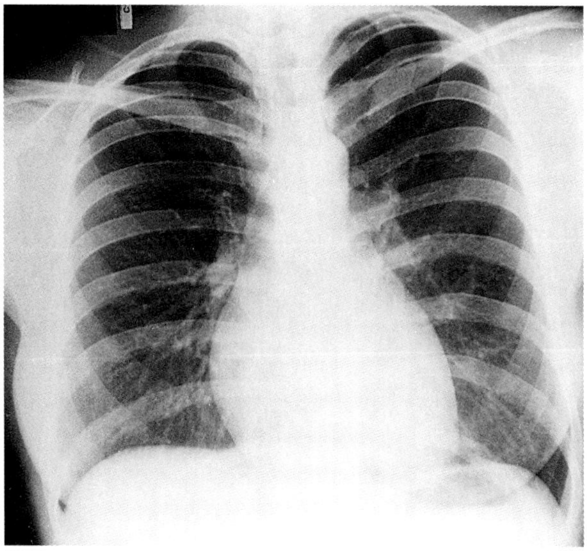

A chest X ray shows the shadow of the heart, lungs, and ribs.

X ray

X rays are one of the most useful forms of energy. Doctors use X rays to make special pictures, called radiographs, of the bones and organs inside the body. Such X-ray pictures help doctors see broken bones, lung disease, or other problems without having to cut into the body. Dentists take radiographs to find tiny cavities in a person's teeth, or to see how the parts of the teeth below the gums look. It takes only a few seconds to make a radiograph, and it does not hurt.

X rays were discovered in 1895 by Wilhelm C. Roentgen, a German scientist. They are a form of energy called electromagnetic radiation. X rays cannot be seen.

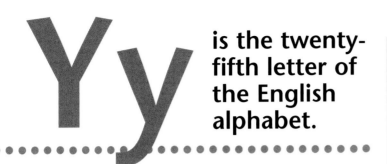

Yy is the twenty-fifth letter of the English alphabet.

Special ways of expressing the letter Y

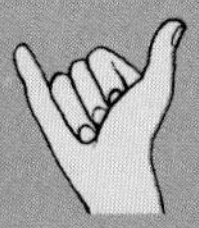

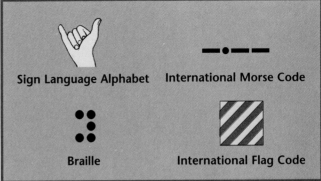

Sign Language Alphabet

International Morse Code

Braille

International Flag Code

Development of the letter Y

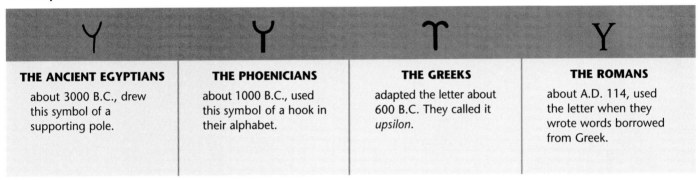

THE ANCIENT EGYPTIANS	THE PHOENICIANS	THE GREEKS	THE ROMANS
about 3000 B.C., drew this symbol of a supporting pole.	about 1000 B.C., used this symbol of a hook in their alphabet.	adapted the letter about 600 B.C. They called it *upsilon.*	about A.D. 114, used the letter when they wrote words borrowed from Greek.

Yak

A yak is a wild ox found in the Asian country of Tibet. Yaks live in high, flat areas, called plateaus (*plah TOHZ*), that are cold and dry.

There are two main kinds of yaks: wild yaks and domestic, or tame, yaks. The wild yak is a big animal covered with black or brownish-black hair. The domestic yak, often called the grunting ox because of the sound it makes, is smaller than the wild yak and easier to handle. It is often white or spotted instead of black.

A yak

Domestic yaks are important to the people of Tibet. They are used as pack animals to carry travelers, mail, and other heavy loads. Also, the people drink yak milk and eat yak meat. They use yak hair to make cloth, mats, and tent coverings.

Yam

Yams are an important food crop in many countries. People cook and eat the tuber (*TOO buhr*), a part of the stem that grows underground.

Yam plants are climbing vines that have small, green flowers. The plants grow in areas with warm, damp weather and a long growing season. Some yams grow up to 6 feet (1.8 meters) long and weigh as much as 100 pounds (45 kilograms). They are white or yellow inside. People often call sweet potatoes yams, because their roots are like yam tubers.

Countries in western Africa produce about half the yams grown each year. Yams also grow in India and in countries of Southeast Asia and the Caribbean Sea.

Yam plants are climbing vines that have small, green flowers, *left.* People cook and eat the tuber, *right,* a part of the stem that grows underground.

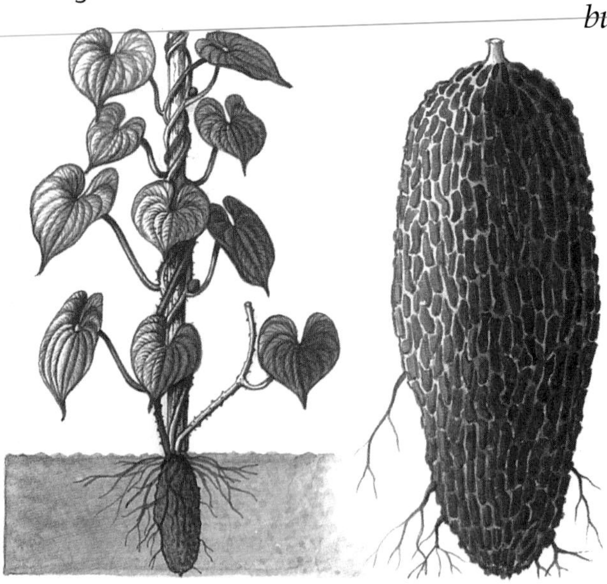

Yangtze River

The Yangtze (*yahng dzuh*) River is the longest and most important river in China. It is also the world's third longest river. Only the Nile River of Egypt and the Amazon River of South America are longer.

The Yangtze River flows through China for 3,900 miles (6,275 kilometers). It begins in the Tanggula Mountains and runs through south-central China to the East China Sea. The river has many twists and turns, so it flows in different directions as it crosses the country.

Small boats carry people and products on the Yangtze. Large ships from the ocean also travel up part of the river. Thousands of Chinese people live on the Yangtze in boats called junks.

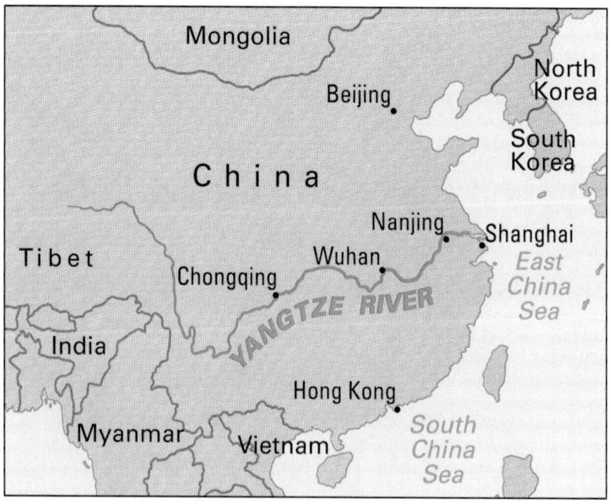

The Yangtze River is China's longest river, and the world's third longest.

Yawning

Yawning is when you open your mouth wide involuntarily and inhale, then exhale. People and animals may yawn when they are sleepy, tired, or bored. Yawning is a sign that the body needs sleep.

Yawning is an involuntary reflex (*REE flehks*)—something your body does by itself, without you having to think about it. Once a yawn starts, it is almost impossible to stop. Even if you close your mouth, the muscles used to yawn continue to contract, or pull. One reason for yawning may be to wake you up by stretching your muscles and helping the blood move around inside your body. Yawning also increases the amount of air you breathe in.

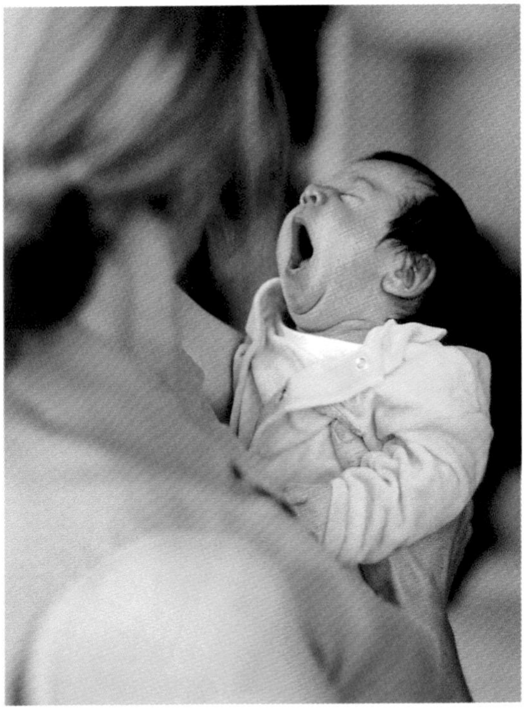

Yawning is a sign that a person needs sleep.

Year

A year is the amount of time it takes Earth to make one complete trip around the sun. A year is 365 days long, plus a few extra hours. Our calendar year is based on this way of measuring a year.

The calendar we use, called the Gregorian calendar, counts only whole days, however. As a result, we have to add one extra day to the calendar every four years to make up for the extra hours that are left over each year. The extra day added is February 29, and a year with that day is called a leap year. Century years—years with even hundreds—are leap years only if they can be divided by 400. Leap years in the late 1900's included 1980, 1984, 1988, 1992, 1996, and 2000. The next leap years will be 2008, 2012, 2016, and every fourth year after that.

In a year, or about 365 days, Earth makes one complete trip around the sun.

Another way of measuring a year is based on the moon, not the sun, and is called the lunar year. The lunar year has 12 lunar months. The ancient Greeks used a lunar year of 354 days. Today, the Chinese use a lunar calendar. A lunar calendar is also used in the religions of Judaism and Islam. The Christian calendar is based partly on the sun and partly on the moon.

Other articles to read: **Calendar; Chinese New Year; New Year's Day; Rosh Ha-Shanah; Season.**

Yeast

Yeast *(yeest)* is a material that bakers put into dough *(doh)* to make it rise. Dough is a mixture of flour and water used to make bread. Yeast is made up of tiny one-celled organisms. As the yeast cells grow in the bread dough, they make the dough puff up, and the baked bread is light and fluffy. Yeast is also used to make beer and wine.

Baker's yeast is produced in two forms—as a moist cake and as dried grains. Cakes of yeast are made up of living, active yeast cells. The cells in dried yeast are alive but not active. Dried yeast must be mixed with warm water before the yeast cells can grow.

Yeast is made up of tiny, one-celled organisms that grow in bread dough and make it puff up.

As more and more yeast cells grow, the dough takes up more and more space. This dough has grown so much it is spilling from the bowl.

Yellowstone National Park

Yellowstone National Park is the oldest national park in the world. It was established in 1872 by the United States government. The park lies in the northwest corner of Wyoming and spreads into Idaho and Montana. It covers several high, flat pieces of land called plateaus (*plah TOHZ*). Mountains rise on the north, east, and west sides of the park. Yellowstone National Park was named for the yellow rocks that lie along the Yellowstone River north of the park.

The park has more hot springs and geysers (*GY zuhrs*) than any other area in the world. A geyser is a hole in the ground that shoots a blast of hot water and steam high into the air. Yellowstone National Park has more than 200 geysers, including the famous "Old Faithful," and thousands of hot springs. Yellowstone also has thundering waterfalls, sparkling lakes, deep canyons, and evergreen forests.

The animals in Yellowstone National Park are protected by law. They include bears, elk, and American buffaloes called bison. Bald eagles, trumpeter swans, and white pelicans build their nests in the park.

More than $2\frac{1}{2}$ million people visit Yellowstone each year. The park has hundreds of miles of trails for walking and horseback riding.

Other articles to read: **Geyser.**

Yellowstone National Park has more geysers and hot springs than any other place on Earth.

Flag

Yemen

Yemen (*YEHM uhn*) is a country in southwestern Asia in the region of the world known as the Middle East. It is near Africa. Yemen lies on the southwestern corner of the Arabian Peninsula. A peninsula is an area of land that is nearly surrounded by water. The Gulf of Aden borders Yemen on the south, and the Red Sea stretches along Yemen's west coast. Saudi Arabia lies north of Yemen, and Oman lies to the east. Sanaa is Yemen's capital and largest city.

Land. Yemen has flatland along the west and south coasts and high hills farther inland. Beyond the highlands, a sandy desert called the Rub al Khali, or Empty Quarter, stretches across the northern border of Yemen into Saudi Arabia.

People. Most of Yemen's people, called Yemenis, are Arab Muslims. They speak Arabic and follow the faith of Islam.

Most Yemenis are farmers or raise animals for a living. Many people sell handmade things, such as cloth, rope, pottery, jewelry, and fancy knives called jambiyas (*jam BEE yuhz*).

City people live in modern houses or apartment buildings, or in one-story brick houses. Some farm families live in towns that have mud-brick houses three or four stories high.

Some Yemenis dress like people in the United States and Europe. Many others wear traditional Arab clothing. The women wear veils and long, dark robes, and the men wear loose shirts with short pants or a skirt called a futa (*FOO tah*). Some men wear tall, round hats called tarbooshes.

Rice, bread, vegetables, lamb, and fish are the main foods in Yemen. The national dish is a spicy stew called salta.

Yemen and its neighbors

Resources and products. Yemen needs help from other countries to support its people. Many young Yemenis work in Saudi Arabia or other nearby countries and send money home to their families.

Farmers in Yemen make money growing khat, a plant with leaves that some people like to chew. Coffee is another important money-making crop. The oil refinery in the port city of Aden uses oil from other countries to make gasoline and other products.

History. Yemen was a center of trade for thousands of years. The queen of Sheba ruled Yemen about 3,000 years ago.

Foreign powers have controlled Yemen for much of its history. The British controlled parts of the country from 1839 into the 1960's. Yemen was supposed to become independent in 1967, but fighting among Arab groups resulted in the creation of two Yemens—North Yemen, with its capital in Sanaa, and South Yemen, with its capital in Aden. In 1990, the two countries joined together to form a single Yemen. But there were still disagreements between northerners and southerners. A short civil war took place in 1994, but the country remained united. In 1999, the people directly elected a president for the first time.

Yemen's capital city, Sanaa, is surrounded by a wall. Traffic leaves and enters through one of eight gates.

Facts About Yemen

Capital: Sanaa.

Area: 203,850 sq. mi. (527,968 km^2).

Population: Estimated 2006 population—21,426,000.

Official language: Arabic.

Climate: Hot and moist along the coast, cooler and wetter in the highlands, hot and dry in the desert. There is little rainfall anywhere in the country.

Chief products:

Agriculture: coffee, fruits, grains, khat (plant leaves), vegetables.

Manufacturing: building materials, handicrafts.

Mining: petroleum.

Form of government: Republic.

A yo-yo is like a top on a string. The player spins the yo-yo out along the string and back again.

Yeti. See **Abominable Snowman.**

Yo-yo

A yo-yo is a small toy that spins on a string. It is made of two round, flat pieces of wood or plastic joined at the center by a small rod, or peg. A string is attached to the peg and winds around it. The person playing with the yo-yo ties the free end of the string to one finger. The yo-yo spins in and out of the hand as the string unwinds and rewinds.

People have had toys like yo-yos for at least 3,000 years. Long ago, people in the Philippines used the yo-yo as a weapon as well as a toy. Yo-yos have been especially popular in the United States and Europe since the 1930's.

Yoga, as well as other exercise, is part of the school day for students at this school in India.

Yoga

Yoga is a set of exercises for the mind and body. It was created by certain followers of the Hindu faith. Their way of thinking is also called yoga, and the people are called yogis or yogins. They use yoga exercises to try to separate the soul from the body and mind. Many people who are not Hindus practice some form of yoga to improve their health and find peace of mind.

Yoga exercises include controlling breathing, silently thinking about a chosen object—and nothing else—for a time, and moving parts of the body into certain positions, or postures *(PAHS chuhrz)*. One of the best-known yoga postures is called the lotus position. This position involves sitting cross-legged with each foot resting on the thigh of the opposite leg. The arms are stretched out, with the wrists resting on the knees, the palms facing up, and the tips of the thumb and first finger pressed together. People often sit in the lotus position to meditate (*MEHD uh tayt*), or relax and think deeply.

Various forms of yoga have become popular in the United States and Europe, though most of the people are not Hindus. Transcendental (*TRAN sehn DEHN tuhl*) Meditation is somewhat like the yoga of Hinduism, only simpler. Hatha-yoga uses difficult body positions and breathing methods to reach better health.

Yogurt

Yogurt (*YOH guhrt*), also spelled *yoghurt,* is a smooth food made from thickened milk. It is a healthful food that provides the same vitamins and minerals as milk.

Yogurt is made by adding certain helpful bacteria, or tiny living things, to milk from cows, goats, buffaloes, or other animals. The bacteria change milk sugar into lactic acid, which makes the milk thicken into yogurt. Lactic acid gives yogurt a sour taste that many people enjoy. Other people like to make yogurt sweeter by adding fruit flavoring.

Yogurt is made from thickened milk.

Yogurt is a popular food in many parts of the world. People in Iran, Turkey, and other countries have eaten yogurt for thousands of years.

HANDS-ON!

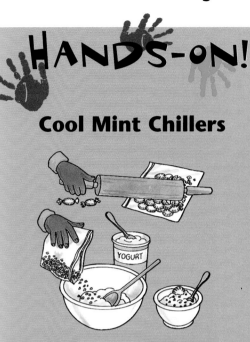

Cool Mint Chillers

This summer yogurt treat is easy to make. Just stir, chill, and enjoy.

If the mints are wrapped, unwrap them. Place them in a plastic bag and seal it. With the rolling pin, pound the mints into chunks. Then roll them into bits.

Empty the yogurt into a mixing bowl. Add the mint pieces and stir.

Pour the mixture into a plastic container. Put the container in the freezer.

After an hour or two, the edges of the yogurt should be frozen. Pour the half-frozen mix into a bowl and stir it again. Pour it back into the container and put it in the freezer. In another hour, your frozen treat should be ready to eat.

Things You Need:

- 1 pound (450 g) of striped mints
- 1 large container of vanilla yogurt
- plastic bag
- mixing bowls
- plastic containers
- rolling pin
- mixing spoon

Yom Kippur

On Yom Kippur, Jews attend religious services and do not eat or work.

Yom Kippur (*YOHM kih POOR*) is the most important Jewish holy day. It is also known as the Day of Atonement. It starts at sunset on the ninth day of the Jewish month of Tishri, which is in September or October, and lasts until the next night.

Yom Kippur is a time when religious Jews think of their sins and ask God to forgive them. They may also ask other people to forgive them. On Yom Kippur, Jews do not eat or work. They spend the day in worship at a temple or synagogue. The books of Leviticus and Numbers in the Bible include the laws of Yom Kippur.

Other articles to read: **Rosh Ha-Shanah.**

Yosemite National Park

Yosemite *(yoh SEHM ih tee)* National Park is a great wilderness in east-central California. It is located in the Sierra Nevada mountains, about 200 miles (320 kilometers) east of San Francisco. It has about 700 miles (1,100 kilometers) of trails. Most of the trails lead to the "High Sierra," a region of sparkling lakes, rushing streams, and jagged mountain peaks.

Yosemite National Park is known for its beautiful scenery, including Lake Yosemite, *shown here,* and Yosemite Falls, *background.*

More than 200 species of birds and more than 60 other kinds of animals live in the forests and mountains. Yosemite has more than 30 kinds of trees and more than 1,300 other kinds of plants.

In 1864, Congress gave Yosemite Valley to California for use as a public park and recreation area. Congress created Yosemite National Park in 1890. Yosemite Valley and the Mariposa Grove were added to the park in 1906.

Many tourists come to the park. Skiing is popular in the High Sierra. Other activities include horseback riding, fishing, golf, tennis, hiking, and swimming.

Young, Cy

Cy Young (1867-1955) was one of the greatest right-handed pitchers in the history of baseball. Young won a record 511 major league games from 1890 through 1911. He also holds the record for the most innings pitched (7,356), the most complete games (753), and the most losses (313). Young pitched for the Cleveland Spiders, St. Louis Nationals, Boston Red Sox, Cleveland Indians, and Boston Braves.

Young was born on March 29, 1867, in Gilmore, Ohio. His full name was Denton True Young. He received the nickname "Cy" after a catcher said he was "as fast as a cyclone." He was elected to the National Baseball Hall of Fame in 1937. He died on Nov. 4, 1955. At the end of each season, the Cy Young Award is given to the outstanding pitcher in the National League and the American League.

Cy Young

Yucatán Peninsula

The Yucatán *(yoo kuh TAN)* Peninsula is a piece of land that separates the Gulf of Mexico from the Caribbean Sea. It includes Mexico's southeastern states of Campeche, Quintana Roo, and Yucatán; nearly all of the country of Belize; and part of El Petén, a section of the country of Guatemala. The peninsula covers over 75,000 square miles (194,000 square kilometers).

Yucatán is a low, slightly hilly land of coral and limestone covered by a thin layer of soil. It has a hot, moist climate. The Mexican city of Cancún, near the tip of the peninsula, is a popular vacation area.

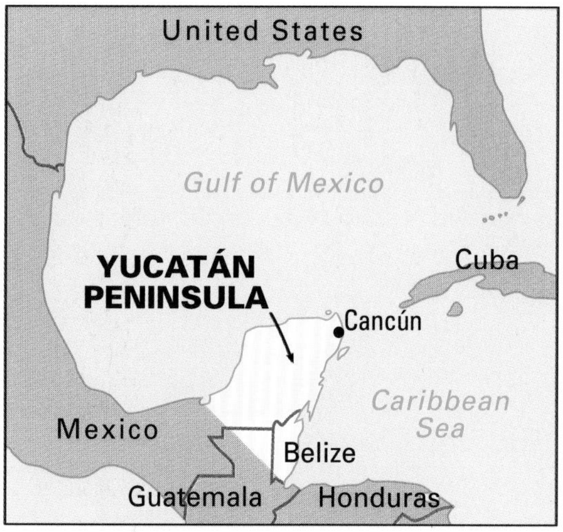

The Yucatán Peninsula

Yukon

Yukon is a section of Canada. It lies in northwest Canada between Alaska and the Northwest Territories. Whitehorse is the capital and largest city of Yukon. It is on the west bank of the Yukon River in the southern part of the territory. More than half of the territory's population lives in Whitehorse.

Land. Yukon is part of a huge region below the Arctic Circle. The Arctic Circle is an imaginary line around the

The Alsek River area in Kluane National Park, Yukon

far northern part of Earth. Yukon has long, cold winters and short, cool summers.

Almost all of Yukon is covered by the Rocky Mountains and other small mountain ranges. There are thick forests of white spruce, birch, fir, pine, and poplar trees. Few people live in Yukon because of its cold climate and rough land.

The Yukon River flows across the territory into Alaska. It is one of the longest rivers in North America. The territory's mountains, lakes, and huge stretches of wilderness make it a popular vacation spot. People who like to fish, camp, and hike go there to enjoy the land.

Resources and products. Yukon has large amounts of minerals. Mining is the most important industry. Zinc is the most valuable mineral product. Gold, lead, and silver are also mined.

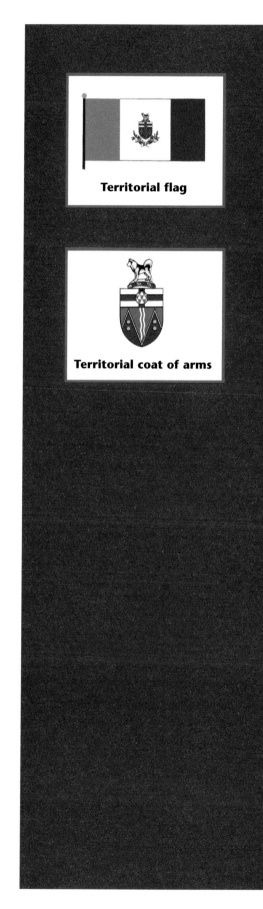

Territorial flag

Territorial coat of arms

Yukon is the smallest of Canada's three territories.

Facts About Yukon

Capital: Whitehorse.

Area: 186,661 sq. mi. (483,450 km²).

Population: 28,674.

Entered the Dominion: 1898.

Territorial abbreviation: YT.

Largest cities: Whitehorse, Dawson.

Government:

Territorial government: Members of the Legislative Assembly: 18.

Federal government: Members of the House of Commons: 1.
Members of the Senate: 1.

Floral emblem
Fireweed

Because of Yukon's short summers, farmers can plant only quick-growing vegetables. Some vegetables are grown in greenhouses—glass or plastic buildings that trap the sun's heat and keep plants warm. Farmers plant hay, too.

Yukon has many small manufacturing industries. Factories make printed materials and metal products. Processing plants make food products, mostly fish. Other industries include chemicals, eyeglass lenses, jewelry, wood products, and American Indian winter coats called Yukon parkas. Yukon also makes money from tourists, or visitors.

History. American Indians have lived in what is now Yukon for thousands of years. The first European people to arrive were English fur traders, in the mid-1800's.

Yukon was owned by the Hudson's Bay Company, a British fur-trading company, until 1870. It was made a district of the Northwest Territories in 1895. In 1898, it became a separate territory.

Yukon is famous for the Klondike Gold Rush. In 1896, gold was found in Bonanza Creek, a branch of the Klondike River. Word of the discovery spread quickly around the world. Thousands of prospectors, or gold diggers, came to the area, hoping to strike it rich. This sudden arrival of newcomers became known as the Klondike Gold Rush of 1897 and 1898.

The Yukon miners were a wild group. The Canadian government had to send the North-West Mounted Police, called the Mounties, to keep order.

Other articles to read: **Alaska Highway; Hudson's Bay Company; Northwest Territories; Rocky Mountains; Yukon River.**

Yukon River

The Yukon River is one of the longest rivers in North America. It begins in Canada, in a series of small lakes in far northwestern British Columbia. Then it flows westward across Canada's Yukon and across Alaska in the United States, where it empties into the Bering Sea. The river's total length is 1,979 miles (3,185 kilometers).

The Yukon River is frozen for up to seven months of the year. Boats can travel on nearly all parts of the river when it is not frozen. In the 1890's, during the early mining days of Alaska and the famous Klondike Gold Rush in Yukon, the river was the main travel route.

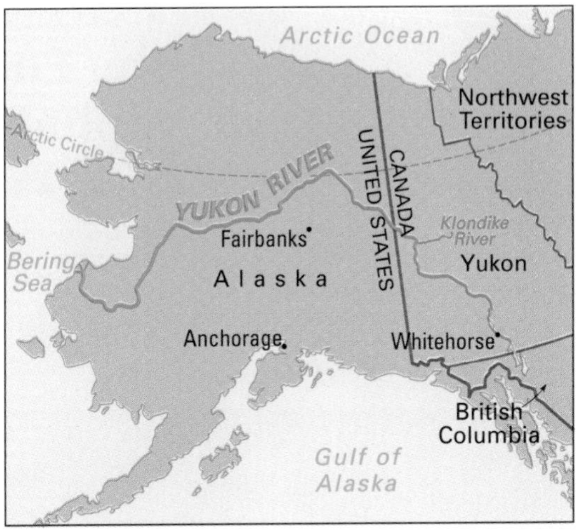

The Yukon River

The Five Finger Rapids on the Yukon River in Canada

Zz is the twenty-sixth letter of the English alphabet.

Special ways of expressing the letter Z

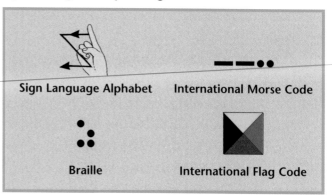

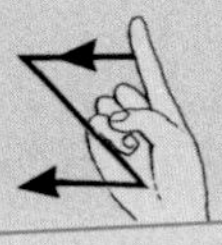
Sign Language Alphabet

International Morse Code

Braille

International Flag Code

Development of the letter Z

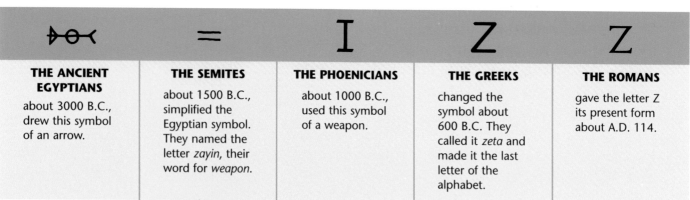

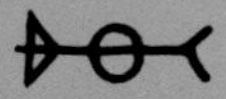	=	I	Z	Z
THE ANCIENT EGYPTIANS about 3000 B.C., drew this symbol of an arrow.	**THE SEMITES** about 1500 B.C., simplified the Egyptian symbol. They named the letter *zayin*, their word for *weapon*.	**THE PHOENICIANS** about 1000 B.C., used this symbol of a weapon.	**THE GREEKS** changed the symbol about 600 B.C. They called it *zeta* and made it the last letter of the alphabet.	**THE ROMANS** gave the letter Z its present form about A.D. 114.

Zaharias, Babe Didrikson

Babe Didrikson Zaharias (*zuh HAIR ee uhs*) (1911?-1956) was an important American golfer. She is generally considered the greatest woman athlete in sports history. She was very good at baseball, basketball, diving, swimming, tennis, and track and field.

Didrikson was born in Port Arthur, Texas. Her real name was Mildred Ella Didrikson. She was nicknamed Babe after the famous baseball player Babe Ruth, because as a child, she hit many home runs like Ruth. She married George Zaharias, a wrestler, in 1938.

Babe Didrikson Zaharias won the U.S. Women's Open golf championship in 1948, 1950, and 1954. In 1950, she helped start the Ladies Professional Golf Association (LPGA).

Babe Didrikson Zaharias is considered the greatest woman athlete in sports history.

Zambia

Zambia *(ZAM bee uh)* is a country in south-central Africa. It is bordered on the north by Congo (Kinshasa) and Tanzania. Malawi and Mozambique lie to the east, Zimbabwe and Namibia lie to the south, and Angola lies to the west. Zambia takes its name from the Zambezi River, which forms most of the country's southern border. Lusaka is Zambia's capital and largest city.

Zambia lies on a high, flat piece of land called a plateau *(plah TOH)*. Most of the country is covered with trees and bushes. Mountains rise in the northeast.

Most of Zambia's people are black Africans who speak a Bantu family language. Many people also speak English, the official language. Most of the people are Christians. Traditional beliefs are important parts of village life.

Many of Zambia's people are farmers. Corn is the country's most important farm product and the people's main food. A favorite dish is nshima *(ehn SHIHM uh)*, a thick porridge made from corn. In the countryside, people live in villages of circular houses with grass roofs. Many people who work in mines live in mining towns. Others hold jobs in government offices or factories.

Zambia is one of the world's largest producers of copper. The nation earns most of its money from selling copper to other countries.

People have lived in what is now Zambia for many thousands of years. People who spoke Bantu family languages arrived in groups between 2,000 and 500 years ago. From 1897 to 1964, the country was called Northern Rhodesia and was controlled by the British. Zambia became independent in 1964.

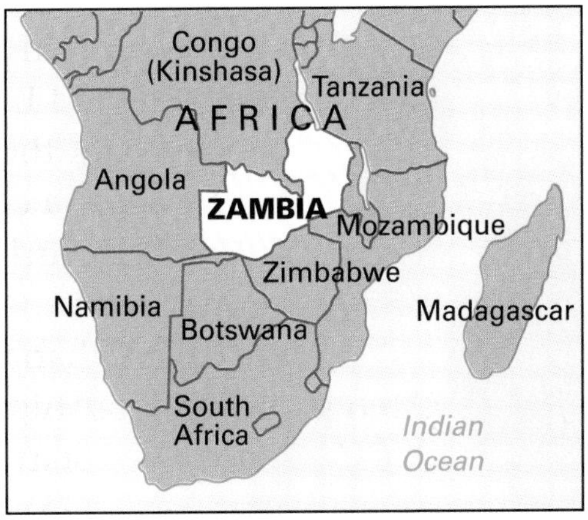

Zambia and its neighbors

Facts About Zambia

Capital: Lusaka.

Area: 290,587 sq. mi. (752,618 km²).

Population: Estimated 2006 population—11,183,000.

Official language: English.

Climate: Warm and dry from May through August; hot and dry from September through November; warm and rainy from November through April.

Chief products:

Agriculture: cassava, corn, millet, sorghum grain, sugar cane.

Fishing: perch, whitebait.

Manufacturing: cement, copper products, flour, wood products.

Mining: cobalt, copper.

Form of government: Republic.

Flag

Emiliano Zapata

Zapata, Emiliano

Emiliano Zapata (*EH mee LYAH noh sah PAH tah*) (1879-1919) was a leader in the Mexican Revolution, which started in 1910. The revolution was a time when several groups fought for control of Mexico. Zapata mainly wanted to get land for his people. He fought first against President Francisco Madero in 1911 and then against General Victoriano Huerta, who took control in 1913.

In 1914, Venustiano Carranza, a state governor, took control away from Huerta. Zapata and the general Pancho Villa took control of Mexico City from Carranza, but the United States helped Carranza stay in power.

Zapata was born in Anenecuilco, Morelos, in Mexico. He was murdered in 1919.

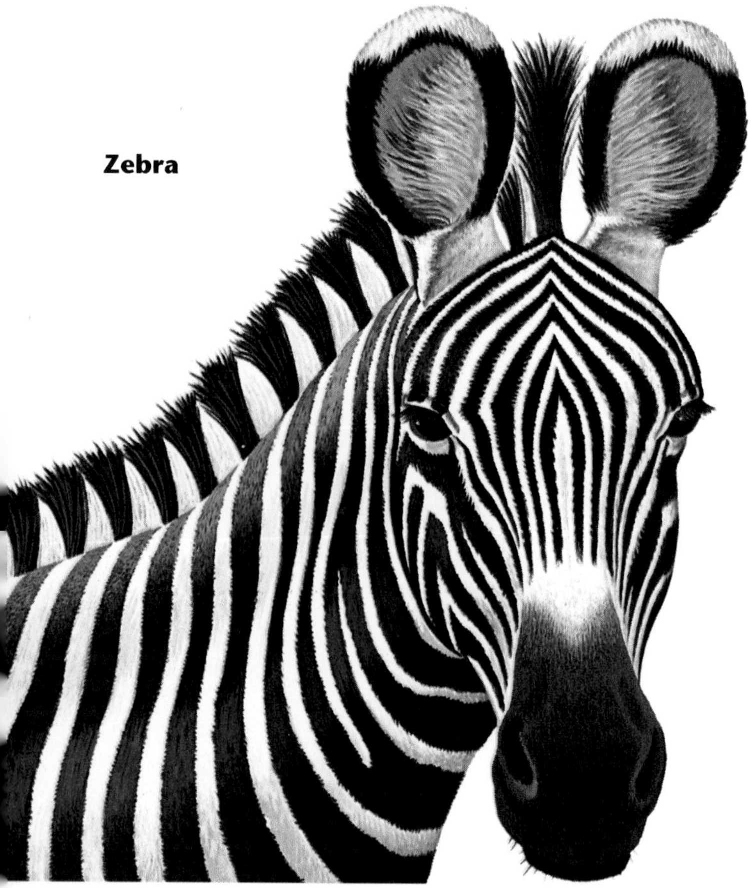

Zebra

Zebra

Zebras are animals that look like horses with stripes. The stripes are white and either black or dark brown. There are three kinds of zebras: the common zebra, Grevy's zebra, and the mountain zebra. All three kinds live in the deserts and grasslands of eastern and southern Africa. Zebras spend most of their time eating. They eat mainly grass.

Zebras live in groups called herds. A herd may have a few zebras or as many as several hundred. Zebras run fast to get away from the lions, hyenas, leopards, and cheetahs that hunt them. Zebras can run as fast as 40 miles (65 kilometers) per hour.

Zeus

Zeus

Zeus (*zoos*) was the king of the gods in the religion of the ancient Greeks. He was the sky and weather god. In Greek art, Zeus is shown as a strong man who has a long beard and often holds a thunderbolt. The Greeks believed that Zeus was an all-knowing and all-seeing father who would protect people.

Zeus lived in a palace on Mount Olympus, a mountain in what is now Greece. He headed a family of 12 major gods and goddesses called the Olympians. He married his sister Hera. Zeus had many children, including the god Apollo and the human hero Heracles, called Hercules by the Romans. The ancient Roman god Jupiter had the same powers as Zeus.

Other articles to read: **Apollo; Hercules; Jupiter.**

Zimbabwe

Zimbabwe (*zihm BAH bway*) is a beautiful country in south-central Africa. Harare is its capital and largest city.

Zimbabwe lies on a high plain called a plateau (*plah TOH*). A famous waterfall called Victoria Falls flows on the Zambezi River along Zimbabwe's northern border.

The largest groups of people that live in Zimbabwe are the Shona and the Ndebele (*ehn duh BEE lee*). These groups have their own languages. Most of Zimbabwe's people also speak English, the official language.

Most of Zimbabwe's people live in the countryside and farm for a living. Corn is the chief crop and the people's main food. The people pound corn into flour to make a dish called sadza or mealies. The people live in houses with grass roofs. Cattle are raised on large ranches.

Zimbabwe is rich in minerals. The nation is an important producer of gold, asbestos, and nickel.

People have lived in what is now Zimbabwe for thousands of years. Around the year 1000, the Shona people built a city with stone walls called Zimbabwe, or Great Zimbabwe, and established a powerful kingdom that lasted for hundreds of years.

From 1897 to 1964, the country was called Southern Rhodesia and was controlled by the British. The country's name became just Rhodesia in 1964. In 1965, Rhodesia became an independent country. For the next 15 years, whites in Rhodesia controlled the government. Fighting took place between black Rhodesians and the government.

In 1980, a new election was held. Blacks won control of the government, and Rhodesia changed its name to Zimbabwe. In the 2000's, the government gave away land owned by white farmers to black farmers. Many white people left the country.

Facts About Zimbabwe

Capital: Harare.

Area: 150,872 sq. mi. (390,757 km²).

Population: Estimated 2006 population—12,975,000.

Official language: English.

Climate: Hot, wet summer from October through April; cool, dry winter from May through September.

Chief products:

Agriculture: cattle, coffee, corn, cotton, fruits, sugar, tea, tobacco, vegetables, wheat.

Manufacturing: chemicals, clothing, food products, iron and steel, metal products, shoes, textiles.

Mining: asbestos, chromite, coal, copper, gems, gold, nickel.

Form of government: Parliamentary democracy.

Flag

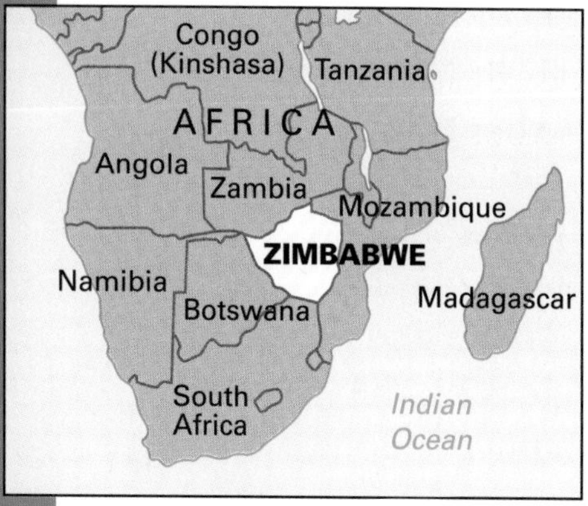

Zimbabwe and its neighbors

Zinc

Zinc is a shiny, bluish-white metal. It is a useful metal that can be bent or molded into a variety of shapes. Such metals as iron and steel are often coated with zinc to keep them from rusting. Zinc-coated metals are used to make roof gutters and other products. Zinc is also used in electric batteries.

Zinc can be combined with other metals to form many mixtures, called alloys. Since 1982, United States pennies have been made from a zinc alloy coated with a thin layer of copper.

Zinc

Zinc is a chemical element. Plants and animals need zinc for normal growth. Many people take vitamins that contain zinc.

Zipper

A zipper is a kind of slide fastener. Zippers are used in many kinds of clothing, especially pants, coats, and boots.

Most zippers have two rows of metal or plastic teeth that lock together. Each tooth has a raised dome on top and a hollow part on the bottom. As the slide is pulled up, it draws the teeth together, one after another, so that the domes fit into the hollows. The teeth stay locked together this way until the slide is pulled down.

The first zipper with locking teeth was invented in 1917. In the 1930's, zippers became common in everyday clothing.

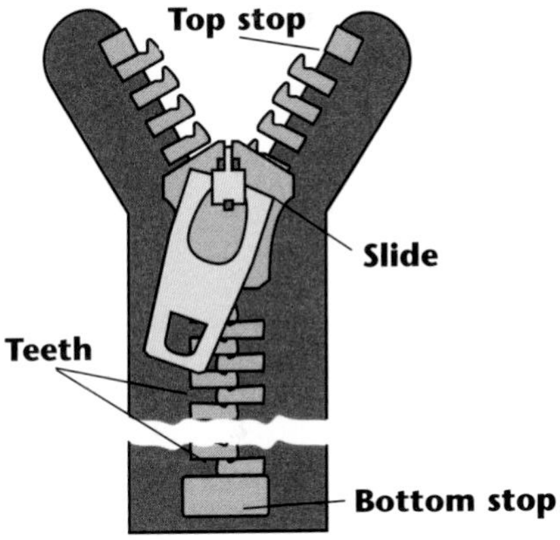

Open-top zipper

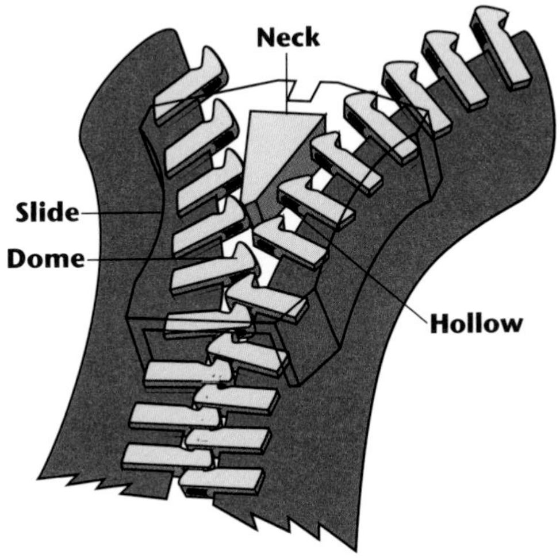

Interior view of slide

Zoo

A zoo is a place where people keep and display, or show, animals. The word *zoo* is short for zoological (*ZOH uh LAHJ uh kuhl*) garden.

People all over the world enjoy visiting zoos. Almost every large city and many smaller towns have a zoo. Many zoos have beautiful gardens with trees along each side of the paths from one animal area to another. Many modern zoos also have gift shops, restaurants, and buildings where people can learn about animals and nature. Some zoos have special areas where children can touch or pet certain animals.

Different zoos keep different kinds of animals. Many large zoos keep mammals, birds, reptiles, and fish from all over the world. Smaller zoos may have just one kind of animal or animals from just one part of the world. Zoos that have only fish and other water animals are called aquariums (*uh KWAIR ee uhmz*).

Some zoos try to group animals in a natural-looking setting. These visitors are watching African animals at the Atlanta Zoo in Georgia.

Why zoos are important

Zoos are important for providing fun and education, saving wildlife, and studying animals. Zoos are fun to visit. People of all ages enjoy looking at animals. In zoos, people can see animals from other parts of the world that they might never see otherwise. Zoos also help people learn how animals live. Many zoos have workers who give tours and teach classes to help people better understand animals' lives.

Saving wildlife has become one of the most important jobs of zoos.

Some animals are in danger of becoming extinct, or dying out, in the wild. Zoos provide a safe place for endangered animals to give birth to their young and increase their numbers.

Zoos are useful places to study animals. The study of animals is called zoology (*zoh AHL uh jee*), and people who study animals are called zoologists (*zoh AHL uh jihsts*). Zoologists study animals in zoos and in the wild to learn more about animal behavior. When zoologists take care of sick animals or study animals that have died, they learn better ways to keep other animals healthy and happy.

Tigers and deer live side by side at the Milwaukee County Zoo in Wisconsin. The deer are safe from the tigers because they are kept apart by a deep moat, or ditch, that visitors cannot see.

Showing the animals

In the past, zoos kept their animals behind steel bars in cages. Today, most zoos no longer use cages. Instead, the animals are placed in large exhibit areas that look like their homes in the wild. These areas have rocks, grass, sand, trees, pools, and places for the animals to rest or hide. The animals are usually separated from the people by a glass wall or by a wide pit called a moat (*moht*).

Many zoos group their animals by type. For example, lions, tigers, and other large cats may be kept in the same building or in nearby outdoor exhibits. Animals that live in the same kinds of areas, such as warm, tropical regions or chilly, snowy places, are often kept together. Zoos also may group animals by the continent where they live in the wild, such as Africa or Asia.

An aquarium is a zoo for water-living animals. At the Sydney Aquarium in Australia, visitors can watch fish and other water animals through an underwater viewing window.

Caring for zoo animals

Trained workers called keepers take care of zoo animals' needs every day. The keepers feed the animals and clean the areas they live in. The food is prepared in a special kitchen. Some animals eat fresh fruits and vegetables. Others, such as the big cats, need raw meat. Snakes eat live rats and mice. Zoos also use prepared pellets, seed mixes, and other foods made especially for animals, somewhat like the foods sold in pet stores.

Most large zoos have at least one veterinarian (*VEHT uhr uh NEHR ee uhn*), or animal doctor, who works at the zoo every day. The veterinarian gives the animals shots to protect them from diseases and takes care of sick animals.

History

People have put wild animals on display for thousands of years. One of the earliest known zoos was established by Queen Hatshepsut (*hat*

SHEHP soot) of Egypt about 3,500 years ago. Emperor Wen Wang of China set up a huge zoo about 3,000 years ago. Soon after that, other rulers in China, India, and northern Africa began to establish small zoos to show off their wealth and power. Rulers and rich people in ancient Greece and Rome also kept private zoos.

Zoos became especially popular in Europe starting in the 1500's, as explorers returned from North and South America with strange new animals that people in Europe had never seen. Small, private exhibits called menageries (*muh NAJ uh reez*) kept a few bears, lions, or tigers in small, gloomy cages. Over the years, menageries were replaced by bigger places with larger collections of animals that got better care. These bigger places were also centers of research. They became the first modern zoos.

The oldest zoo that is still open today is the Schönbrunn Zoo in Vienna, Austria. It was started in 1752. Other old zoos that are still open are in Madrid, Spain (started in 1775); Paris (1793); and Berlin, Germany (1844). The first zoo in the United States opened in Philadelphia in 1874. Canada's first zoo opened in Halifax, Nova Scotia, in 1847.

In 1907, Karl Hagenbeck, a German zoo owner, began using moats instead of cages to separate animal display areas from visitors. The idea slowly spread to zoos throughout the world. In the 1940's, zoos began to keep groups of endangered animals to save them from dying out.

Other articles to read: **Animal; Endangered species; Zoology.**

Zoo animals need care from a doctor or dentist, just as people do. This Siberian tiger has been given a medicine to make it sleep while its teeth are checked by a veterinarian.

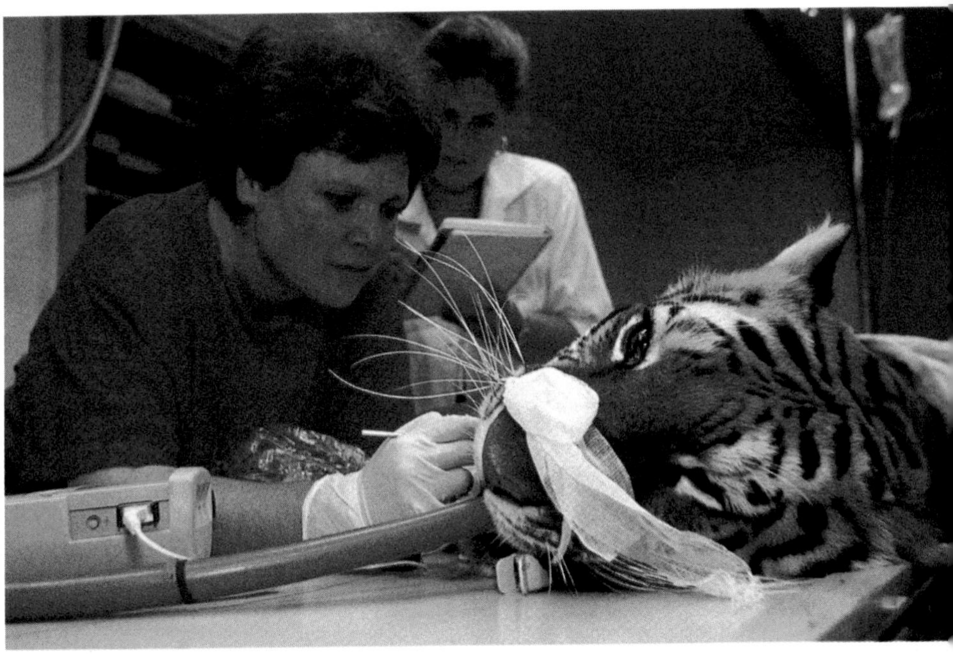

Zoology

Zoology (*zoh AHL uh jee*) is the study of animals. People who study animals are called zoologists (*zoh AHL uh jists*). Zoologists study how animals eat, sleep, play, mate, and give birth to their young. Zoologists watch how animals act toward one another and how they fit in with their surroundings. The scientists learn how different kinds of animals are related to one another and how certain animals have changed over time. Zoologists also try to figure out what effects animals have on people and what effects people have on animals.

Zoologists study animals. This zoologist is gathering information about a deer at a zoo.

Some zoologists work in zoos. Some work in modern laboratories at universities, research centers, and museums. Other zoologists study animals outdoors. Many branches of zoology deal with a particular kind of animal. For example, entomology (*ehn tuh MAHL uh jee*) is the study of insects, the largest group of animals.

The study of zoology has helped people in many ways. Human beings have many body parts that work like those of other animals. So zoologists often study animals to better understand human health and medicine. Zoologists also try to find ways of dealing with harmful insects and worms.

In 1758, the Swedish zoologist Carolus Linnaeus (*KAR uh luhs lih NEE uhs*) created a system to classify, or group, animals. With his system, scientists all over the world could use the same scientific name for a kind of animal. Thus, it became easier to keep track of all the different kinds.

Other articles to read: **Animal.**